Régis Deb

A Critical Intro

Keith Reader

Pluto Press

LONDON • EAST HAVEN, CONNECTICUT

First published 1995 by Pluto Press
345 Archway Road, London N6 5AA
and 140 Commerce Street,
East Haven, Connecticut 06512, USA

99 98 97 96 95 5 4 3 2 1

British Library Cataloguing in Publication Data
A catalogue record for this book is available from the British Library

ISBN 0 7453 0821 X hbk

Library of Congress Cataloging in Publication Data
Reader, Keith.
Régis Debray: a critical introduction/Keith Reader.
p. cm. — (Modern European thinkers)
Includes bibliographical references and index.
ISBN 0–7453–0821–X. — ISBN 0–7453–0822–8 (pbk.)
1. Debray, Régis—Political and social views. 2. Ex-Communists —France—Attitudes. 3. France—Politics and government—1981– 4. Mass media—Political aspects—France. 5. France—Cultural policy. 6. Intellectuals—France—Attitudes. 7. World politics—1989– I. Title. II. Series.
HX264.R43 1995
335.43—dc20 95–14373
CIP

Designed and produced for Pluto Press by
Chase Production Services, Chipping Norton, OX7 5QR
Typeset from disk by Stanford DTP Services
Printed in the EC by T J Press, Padstow, England

Régis Debray

Modern European Thinkers

Series Editor: Professor Keith Reader (Kingston University)

The Modern European Thinkers series offers low-priced introductions for students and other readers to the ideas and work of key cultural and political thinkers of the post-war era.

For a complete list of available titles please contact the Pluto Press office.

To my mother

Contents

Introduction

The name of Régis Debray is a familiar one in some parts of the world, but all too often for reasons which have little or nothing to do with what I shall argue to be the longer-term importance of his work. The usually astute Sunil Khilnani, writing in the British newspaper the *Guardian* of 26 April 1994, referred to de Gaulle as 'bugbear of the Left during his reign, and now darling to Régis Debray and others of the greying 1968 generation' – a judgement in which only the 'greying' is incontestably true. Debray spent 1968 in a Bolivian prison, and ten years after the May events produced a text (*Modeste contribution aux discours et célébrations du dixième anniversaire/A Modest Contribution to the Discourses and Celebrations of the Tenth Anniversary*) highly critical of assumptions that they represented a possibility for the revolutionary overthrow of French capitalism. His admiration for de Gaulle is, as I shall show, a selective and polemical one, focusing as it does Debray's attachment to the institutions of the republic and the state and to a verbal culture he sees as jeopardised by the omnipresence of the visual.

The kind of misrepresentation of Debray suggested by Khilnani's choice of phrase sometimes goes so far as to construct his career as a paradigmatic, or even parodic, move across the political spectrum – from 'revolutionary leftist', through Mitterrandist, to some kind of disabused position on the right.

Only the second of these assertions, and then primarily during the first Mitterrand term of office, has any truth about it. Debray was indeed engaged in revolutionary activity with Che Guevara in Latin America, but has never believed violent political revolution to be desirable or possible in the West; and his hostility to the French right (as to many of the 'champagne socialists' whose opportunism he had occasion to know only too well) remains contemptuously unremitting. An accurate description of his development would be from theoretician, and briefly practitioner, of revolution in Latin America, through critic of the media's sway over intellectual and cultural life in France and staunch defender of the state and republican values, to philosopher, anthropologist and historian of the interrelationship between media and social formations – 'mediologue', to use his own preferred term. The movement away from the political figured here does not mean a movement away from contemporary reality, but rather an extension and refinement of the framework he uses to engage with it.

The Debray to be met in these pages is thus a very different character from the 'Robin Hood' of myth – more sardonic, more philosophical, an evolving intellectual presence rather than a moustachioed time-warp. Much of his work (notably *Les Masques*) is also to be situated in a very important French tradition of first-person autobiographical or self-reflective writing whose antecedents include Montaigne, Rousseau, Stendhal and Michel Leiris. I have made less of this than perhaps I might have done, simply because I suppose only the minimum of educated familiarity with France in my readership.

If Debray's work is so little known or understood in English-speaking countries, this is in large measure because so little of it has been translated (and much is out of print even in French). I have therefore included substantially more direct quotation from the original texts than would have been appropriate for an author (such as Michel Foucault) readily accessible to an English-speaking audience. There is a clear need for something like a 'Debray reader'; this is not it, but I hope that it will go some way towards filling that gap.

Translations from the French (in all cases except where otherwise indicated) are my own. I have offered an English translation of the title of each work (and where appropriate the title under which the English translation was published) after the French when reference is first made to it. Titles thereafter are given in French.

Finally, some thanks are in order. Kingston University Human Sciences Research Fund provided funds for me to spend part of the summer of 1992 researching this book in Paris. The University Human Sciences Computer Unit and Tony Brown dealt admirably and efficiently with technical glitches with which I was incapable of coping. Trevor Jones introduced me to Anne Beech at Pluto, who was a fountain of good advice and reassurance. My warmest thanks, however, go to Régis Debray himself. To write about the work of a living human being is not the easiest of undertakings; he made it much easier, providing information and cooperation unstintingly and never seeking to exercise any species of 'editorial control' even where our disagreements were most evident. I hope that this work will help to make his work better known to an English-speaking public than it has hitherto been.

Keith Reader
April 1995

CHAPTER 1

The Latin American Years

Régis Debray's involvement with the liberation struggles in Latin America, which provide the context and setting for his early fictional text *La Frontière/The Frontier*, catapulted him into worldwide prominence in 1967, when he was arrested whilst travelling, under his own name and in civilian clothes, as a journalist in Bolivia and sentenced to thirty years' imprisonment. Pleas for clemency from many leading figures (including General de Gaulle and Jean-Paul Sartre, significantly – in view of Debray's subsequent evolution – on the same side for once) were ignored, and it was not until after a counter-coup, led by General Torres, against the Bolivian military junta that he was released on 23 December 1970. To this day and despite major changes in his fields of activity, Debray's name, as suggested in the Introduction, remains for most who know it indelibly associated with those of Fidel Castro and Ernesto 'Che' Guevara. He has made it clear that his commitment to the Cuban revolution in no way implied an endorsement of the country's internal structures; it represented simply a championing of the Castro régime's democratic right to exist in the face of United States' economic and military pressure. I shall be attempting in this chapter not only to give a succinct account of Debray's work – theoretical, polemical and fictional – about or set in Latin America, but to place his involvement in the social and cultural context of its time.

That context, for Debray, had been in the first instance the ideologically and politically charged world of 1960s' intellectual Paris. Born on 2 September 1940 of right-wing parents – lawyers who were to be active in the Resistance – he won the Concours Général prize for philosophy at the age of sixteen; a photograph depicts him receiving the award from the vice-president of the Paris municipal council – his mother. The Concours Général, which goes back to 1744, is a competitive examination for the French equivalent of sixth-formers, judged by a specialised national jury in each discipline. It has no direct effect on candidates' future careers, but its very existence, and the attention it annually attracts, give some indication of the intense competitiveness of academic life in France and the prestige in which scholastic achievement there is held. It was entirely consonant with this early success that Debray should have gone on to the prestigious Lycée Louis le Grand and thence to the École Normale Supérieure.

This institution (familiarly known as 'Normale Sup') was founded by the Revolutionary Convention in 1794 to identify and educate the *crème de la crème* of the young French intelligentsia. Admission is by competitive examination (Debray produced the best of his year in 1959), and students enjoy exceptionally favourable material and intellectual conditions in which to prepare for yet another competitive examination – the *agrégation*, success in which is necessary to guarantee a post in a university or a top *lycée*. 'Normale Sup' in many ways resembles Oxford or Cambridge, with both of which it maintains close links, but even more than these institutions is, first and foremost, a nursery for intellectuals, who have included such figures as Léon Blum, Michel Foucault, Jean Jaurès, Jean-Paul Sartre and Simone Weil.

It is not innocent that the five names I have mentioned are all in different ways associated with political positions of the left. The École Normale has a long tradition of left-wing political involvement, traceable back to Lucien Herr (its librarian at the turn of the century and a prominent socialist), and beyond that doubtless to the circumstances of its foundation. The French Revolution was as strikingly as, and more enduringly than, its Russian successor, a political and ideological word made flesh, the putting into action of the philosophies of liberty, equality and fraternity articulated by such Enlightenment thinkers as Diderot and Rousseau.[1] The structural centrality this gave the French intelligentsia (to use a term of twentieth-century invention) was reinforced by the Dreyfus affair of 1894, for it was largely thanks to the self-styled 'intellectuals' manifesto', published in 1898, that the case was reopened and Dreyfus's innocence proclaimed. A leading figure in that campaign was Lucien Herr; another was Léon Blum, who in 1936 was to become prime minister in the Socialist-led Popular Front government.[2] The figure that after World War Two most clearly embodied the École Normale's connection with left-wing ideas was the philosopher Louis Althusser, whose relationship with the institution dated from his arrival there as a student in 1945 through to his internment in a psychiatric hospital in 1980.

Althusser became a committed Marxist, like so many others, as a result of his experiences in the War, and remained throughout his active life a member of the French Communist Party, and its leading intellectual. That he was Debray's philosophy tutor at Normal Sup is of considerably more than anecdotal interest. For one thing, Debray speaks with exceptional warmth of Althusser's erudition and dedication to his pupils, thereby helping to place in their rightful context – that of the delirium of a mind at the end of its tether – the repeated 'admissions' in Althusser's autobiographical *L'Avenir dure longtemps/The Future Lasts a Long Time* that he had never properly read many of the texts he taught or wrote about.

For another, and more centrally, Althusser's intellectual influence is strikingly manifest in Debray's work on Latin America. The 1960s marked a period (in fact inaugurated by Khrushchev's denunciation of Stalin at the Soviet Communist Party's congress in 1956) in which not only the analytical focus of much of the Marxist left, but also its emotional investment – its constitution of objects of social and political desire – shifted away from the USSR. This was obviously not true of the French Communist Party, which remained the most pro-Soviet in Western Europe; but the new lefts that were to find their moment of glory in 1968 looked much more readily to on the one hand Asia (Mao's China and the struggle in Vietnam), and on the other Latin America (Castro's Cuba and the example of Ernesto 'Che' Guevara) for their inspiration.

For all his continuing (and often sorely tried) loyalty to the Communist Party, Althusser's work was profoundly influenced by the philosophical writings of Mao Ze-dong, in particular the essay *On Contradiction*. Mao's espousal of the principle of contradiction as 'the basic law of nature and society and therefore also the basic law of thought'[3] is developed in Althusser's influential essay 'Contradiction et surdétermination/Contradiction and overdetermination' to produce a determinedly anti-Hegelian – hence, for Althusser, anti-idealist – reading of Marx, seen as urgently necessary to restore to the Communist movement the theoretical vigour and rigour it had lost in the Stalinist years.[4] The Third World thus constituted a major influence upon, rather than a mere receptacle for, Western Marxist theory, much as it was to become for Debray a few years later.

Where Althusser most sharply diverged from the dominant trend in the French Communist Party of his day (reaching its apotheosis at the 1976 Conference which removed from the Party's programme all reference to the dictatorship of the proletariat) was in his staunch adherence to the Leninist tradition. This, now almost universally discredited, evolved as a response to the repressiveness of Tsarist Russia and laid quasi-absolute stress on the rigorous organisation of a vanguard party, in particular on democratic centralism (whereby once the party line had been decided by democratic debate and the taking of a vote all members, whether or not personally favourable to it, were required to abide by it in all their activity).

Leninism, as befitted the creation of a lawyer, gave a privileged place to intellectuals, for 'the working class, exclusively by its own efforts, is able to develop only trade-union consciousness',[5] and it is for the revolutionary socialist intelligentsia to place their education at the service of the movement and its theoretical development.

Althusser's unceasing stress on the paramountcy of theory, like his adherence to what he always felt to be the only party of the French working class, clearly derives from the Leninist tradition. His influence in the French left-wing intellectual world, through his position at the École Normale Supérieure, was immense, and probably more than any other factor accounts for the strength of first Communist, then Maoist ideas in that institution (where Trotskyism, the other major force on the French New Left, was never so powerful).

Debray joined the Communist Party's student wing – the only political party to which he has ever belonged – whilst at Normale Sup and remained a member until 1963. In his *Prison Writings*, he was to reflect wryly on the isolationism and cultural bias of that movement ('We could barely conceive the possibility that other cultures, climates or temperaments might ever produce models of any other kind').[6] Yet I shall argue that the fusion of Third World influence and a Leninist organisational philosophy implicit in the Althusserian project was to recur, in a very different form, in Debray's first major writings. Hartmut Ramon's observation that Debray's *Revolution in the Revolution?* consists of '... highly structured, rigorous arguments and a body of empirical theses (the listing of chains of 'theses' is a favourite literary device of Althusser's)'[7] suggests how this recurrence manifests itself.

First, however, let us look at why this happened. Debray had visited the United States in the summer of 1959 and returned via Cuba, where Castro had taken power after a protracted and resourceful guerrilla campaign; he and Guevara had entered Havana, with symbolic appropriateness, on 1 January. Debray returned there in the summer of 1961, meeting Castro for the first time, and in 1963 and 1964 visited every Latin American country with the exception of Paraguay, staying with the FALN guerrilla group in Venezuela. The attraction of the liberation struggles in Latin America at that time is easily understood, especially bearing in mind that the Vietnam war – as it were an alternative focus for revolutionary ardour – was not to break out until August 1964.

Castro's guerrilla campaign against the US-backed Batista dictatorship, which had begun in earnest with the landing of eighty-two men on 2 December 1956, had the romantic appeal of David taking on Goliath, coupled with that of a Marxism learnt in action, on the ground (Castro compared his discovery of it to finding a map in a forest), rather than in the rarefied atmosphere of Latin Quarter seminars. The Althusserian insistence on the importance of theory and the conviction that 'the duty of every revolutionary is to make the revolution' (the quotation is from Castro's Second Havana Declaration, but would not have come amiss from the Sartre of the time) fused in an exhilarating archetype of revolutionary theoretical practice.

It is little wonder that, in what now appears as the interregnum between the end of the Algerian war and the protests against Vietnam which, along with a host of other things, were to culminate in the May 1968 events, the Latin American guerrilla struggle held such powerful, and not merely exotic, appeal. As important a figure as Castro in accounting for this appeal was 'Che' Guevara.

Guevara's writings were a major influence on Debray (it could almost be said that he played the same role in introducing them to the Western intelligentsia as Althusser did for Mao), and his killing after a CIA-organised Bolivian ambush in October 1967 gave him enduring mythical importance as a true martyr to the revolutionary cause. The hagiographic – not to say Christological – tone in which he was so often alluded to was, considering the importance of radical Catholics such as the Peruvian Gustavo Gutiérrez (apostle of liberation theology) in the Latin American struggles, hardly inappropriate, and found much of its justification in his celebrated maxim that 'the true revolutionary is guided by feelings of love'.[8]

That love, however, was only effective if translated into action, an action that crucially for Debray needed to be national and international at one and the same time. Guevara, an Argentine national, became a key member of Castro's government in Cuba before leaving in 1965 to participate in revolutionary struggles abroad. His endeavour to 'create one, two, a hundred Vietnams' led him first to the Congo, then to Bolivia and his death. Such an ideologically committed internationalism was, and could only have been, effective in practice because it was grounded in a firm grasp of the geographical, historical and political realities of the individual nations it embraced. The rallying-cry 'Patria o muerte!' ('Homeland or death!') with which so many of Guevara and Castro's speeches concluded was – is – more than a rhetorical signing-off flourish. Cuba for Guevara was not merely a (literal) island of socialist hope in a continent that for 500 years and more had been a milch-cow for Spanish, Portuguese and American imperialism. It was also an example to be followed in the other countries that made up that continent, and an example that (*mutatis mutandis* like that of the USSR for the European left at one time) showed that revolutionary situations could arise at times and in places quite different from what might have been predicted.

Guevara drew three fundamental conclusions from the Cuban revolution, conclusions that were to have a profound effect on Debray's thinking. These were that:

1. Popular forces can win a war against an army.

2. One does not necessarily have to wait for a revolutionary situation to arise; it can be created.
3. In the under-developed countries of the Americas, rural areas are the best battlefields for revolution.[9]

The most abidingly false of Marx's historical predictions has always been that revolution will be essentially an urban phenomenon, coming about in advanced industrial societies. This was no more true of Russia in 1917 or of China in 1949 than it was of Cuba in 1959, and on each of those occasions Marxist theory needed to be expanded and rewritten to take different circumstances into account.

Guerrilla warfare, which had already proved its efficacy in fomenting the Chinese revolution, involved small, dedicated groups of what Guevara called 'agrarian revolutionaries', using their developed knowledge of the terrain and of its inhabitants to extend and develop their support among the population.

The guerrilla base in Latin America was known as a *foco* – a Spanish word meaning 'focal point' – and represented at once the heart of the revolutionary struggle and the locus of its major contradictions. Foremost among these latter was that between the city and the countryside. The Leninist theory of revolution was implicitly at least an urban one, depending as it did on the combination of the industrial working class and trained intellectual cadres.

Cities in most Latin American countries, however, were dangerous places, heavily infiltrated by the CIA; it was not for nothing that Castro and Guevara delayed their entry into Havana until Batista had fled and their triumph was assured. Given that the fundamental rallying-cry of all Latin American national liberation movements was for land reform, the countryside seemed the most appropriate as well as the safest place for the revolutionary to be, as Mao famously proclaimed, 'like a fish in water'.

Guevara's treatise on *Guerrilla Warfare* is an amalgam of coldly sober realism (expressed in suggestions about what supplies to take and weapons to use, as well as in such injunctions as 'Do not execute anyone without a hearing unless the situation permits no other alternative')[10] and exalting rhetoric ('Any army so welded to the people – the peasants and workers from whom it sprang – an army so conversant with strategy and ideologically secure, such an army is invincible').[11] Its textual practice combines 'rural' topographical knowledge with the 'urban' theoretical assurance required by the revolution, and was enacted by Guevara in his own life.

It should also be borne in mind in this context that the Cuban revolution began as a national liberation struggle. Not until 1 May 1961 – into its third year – was it proclaimed to be socialist, and not until 2 December of that same year, doubtless for reasons not unconnected with the USSR's readiness to buy much of the Cuban sugar crop, did Castro describe himself as a Marxist-Leninist. This was a long way from Lenin's return to the Finland Station in 1917 to take power and thereby enter into his ideological inheritance.

Marxism – Leninist or not, about which more will shortly be said – grew out of the Cuban revolution rather than inspiring it from the start, and this inevitably meant that revolutionary struggles elsewhere in Latin America, much as they looked to Cuba for support and inspiration, were at the same time deeply rooted in national specificities of their own.

The romantic vision of the footsore bearded hero (and prospective martyr), on the march through an area whose population may or may not appreciate what he is doing for them, frequently undernourished and with only his rifle and the works of Fidel for protection, is thus not the whole story. It needs to be offset by a view at once more pragmatic, depending as it does on close knowledge of the area of struggle, and wider-ranging, for in this of all political situations (as Mao and Castro had both proved) a numerically insignificant vanguard can quite literally come to determine the future of a nation and conceivably even a continent.

The title of *Revolution in the Revolution?* refers to the impact of the guerrilla strategy upon Western Marxist notions of how revolutionary change would come about. After passing his philosophy *agrégation* in 1965, Debray went to Cuba – ostensibly as visiting professor of the history of philosophy at the University of Havana, in practice to observe and train with the guerrillas in their camps – in January 1966. He had already produced his first major text, the essay *Le Castrisme: la longue marche de l'amérique latine/Castroism: the Long March in Latin America*, whose orientation towards a Western audience is shown by the fact that it was published in *Les Temps Modernes* and *New Left Review* in 1965 before appearing in the Cuban magazine *Casa de las Américas*.

This essay opens with homage to the militants from whom Debray had learnt and, importantly, to the individual countries – Venezuela, Colombia, Ecuador, Peru, Bolivia, Argentina, Uruguay, Brazil – in which their struggles were taking place, followed by a warning against 'conferring the allure of the exceptional on what are everyday events in contemporary South America' and a reference to Althusser's insistence that '"no tactic is possible which does not rest on some strategy and no strategy which does not rest on some theory"'.[12] The juxtaposition of Western Marxist theses with intimate local and national knowledge, and the studied avoidance of the Eurocentric exoticism that so often blurred analyses of events in Latin America and Asia alike, are all thoroughly characteristic of Debray's approach, and in one form or other recur throughout the body of his work.

Castroism (as I shall hereinafter refer to it for brevity) insistently warns against excessive spontaneity and the myth of the *coup d'état*, criticised for leaving existing institutions – bureaucratic, financial and military – unchanged. Like so much in Debray's Latin American writings, this is Leninist without at first appearing to be so. In *State and Revolution*, Lenin stresses that 'the working class must break up, smash the "ready-made state machinery", and not confine itself merely to taking control of it'[13] – along with the vanguard party his most influential contribution to Marxist theory, and taken in the West as a warning against parliamentary or electoral roads to socialism.

In most Latin American countries, however, democratic institutions were fragile or non-existent, so that the *coup d'état* had long been the standard method of changing the régime, structurally the equivalent of the electoral process in the West. Debray's warnings against it and counter-advocacy of the *foco* thus in turn correspond to Lenin's espousal of the vanguard party and violent revolution against 'parliamentary cretinism', reinscribing the Leninist problematic into the conditions of another continent.

At a time when Leninism's political future appears well and truly behind it, the relevance of this analysis may be called into question. It is, summarily, that Debray is and has always been a Western, and more particularly a Parisian, intellectual, formed by, as he has gone on to form, the particular kind of education or 'mentality'* – at once deeply theoretically committed and committed to intervention in specific contexts – of which Althusser but also in their different ways Sartre and Bourdieu are symptomatic.[14] The view – abetted, doubtless unconsciously, by the romantic dash of his Zapata moustache – that the Debray of the 'Latin American years' represented some kind of Tolstoyan disowning of this intellectual tradition and existential drowning of the guilt of privilege in altruistic revolutionary action would thus be very wide of the mark. A universal grammar of socio-political action (which is what any serious Marxism has claimed to be) is valid only if applicable in – thus, modified by – this or that highly specific context. This is why 'Fidelism', for Debray, is not really an ideology at all, but rather 'the concrete process of the regeneration of Marxism and Leninism in Latin American conditions and according to the historic traditions of each country';[15] and *Castroism*, with its detailed analyses of the different national situations and insistence that 'each national variant of Fidelism will draw a revolutionary inspi-

* I use this term as the best available rendition of the French *mentalité*, used by writers as different as the Annales school of historians or the sociologist Pierre Bourdieu to designate a transindividual, generally class- or historically-bounded approach to symbolic phenomena.

ration from its own tradition of national independence struggles',[16] is a constant reminder of this.

Each national liberation struggle part of that of a continent, that continent's in its turn part of that of the whole of capitalist society: the specificity of Debray's analyses, matched by the grandeur of their sweep, leads him to conclude that the new societies in Latin America will be built upon 'that alliance of the Promethean lyricism of revolutionary action ... and a pitiless lucidity with respect to its own efforts ... symbolised with such mythic perfection in the encounter of two men: the Cuban Fidel Castro and the Argentinian Che Guevara'.[17]

Things did not, of course, turn out as Debray predicted. Yet to those who would mock the passage's élan it is worth retorting that at the time of writing (1994) fewer Latin American countries are under the rule of military juntas than ever before. To write about Latin America of all places is almost by definition to give a hostage to fortune, but there has been an undoubted democratisation of the continent (facilitated as much by the ineptitude of many of the military régimes as by any shining revolutionary example), whilst the still pervasive force of myth in its political life is currently graphically illustrated by the example of Jean-Bertrand Aristide in Haiti. Debray's conclusion to *Castroism* may be excessively sanguine, but it had a degree of predictive force and continues to be of relevance.

In *Amérique Latine: quelques problèmes de stratégie révolutionnaire/Problems of Revolutionary Strategy in Latin America*, which appeared in the École Normale Supérieure-published *Cahiers Marxistes-Léninistes* in 1965, Debray gives a more explicitly political overview of the relationship between Cuba and struggles elsewhere in Latin America. The 'Balkanisation' of South America ('still not a continent',[18] because of the largely US-inspired division and ignorance between struggles in one nation and another) is adduced as a major reason why the Cuban example had spread in less wildfire fashion than had been hoped. Cuba's geographical isolation, intensified by the economic and political manoeuvrings of imperialism (only Mexico among Latin American governments at the time Debray was writing still had diplomatic relations with Havana), maintained 'the backwardness and division of revolutionary parties in Latin America', for 'a socialist revolution also revolutionizes counter-revolution'.[19]

Cuba brought about a qualitative transformation in the Latin American class struggle, at once rehabilitating Marxism and showing the inadequacy of earlier variants of it not solidly anchored in national reality. But this transformation paradoxically led to at least short-term gains for imperialism, whose mind it wonderfully concentrated and which in consequence was not slow to reinforce and extend its machinery of oppression and in many countries to unite bourgeois, counter-revolutionary forces against the 'socialist threat'.

Debray has sharp words for the 'reformist' strategy adopted notably in Chile, for which in terms that echo Althusser 'the "theoretical humanism" of Marxism serves to justify the abandonment of all political and theoretical rigour.'[20] The victory of the right in the 1964 elections is squarely attributed to the pacific soft-pedalling of the FRAP (the leftist 'popular front' alliance), and there seems a hideous prefiguration of the 1973 coup in Debray's assertion that 'an electoral result which represented an electoral victory unequalled in Latin America by any other "democratic movement" was turned into a revolutionary defeat'.[21]

For Debray, a bourgeois-democratic revolution in Latin America (as in 1917 Russia, or still more pertinently in 1959–61 Cuba) is impossible without leading to a socialist one, so that pace Allende and the FRAP 'the alternative today is not between (peaceful) bourgeois revolution and (violent) socialist revolution ... but between revolution tout court and counter-revolution'.[22] Here, clearly, we are back with *State and Revolution*, so that Debray's conclusion that 'Fidelism is none other than Leninism'[23] comes as no surprise. Hartmut Ramon was to observe in 1978 that Debray effected a synthesis of Guevarism, Leninism and Althusserianism;[24] if Guevarism is taken as practically coterminous with Fidelism, and Althusser's insistent reinscription of Lenin borne in mind, it might better be said that he brought out or clarified a synthesis that was always already there.

Althusser is invoked again in *Le Rôle de l'Intellectuel/The Role of the Intellectual*, like the other texts we have been considering published along with *Révolution dans la révolution?* in France. This evokes the context of the opposition between militancy and intellectual activity for so long dominant in the West (as sneers at 'armchair revolutionaries' have periodically gone to show) and often seen as overcome in Latin America, above all in the persons of Castro and Guevara. Althusser is praised for having been 'a militant at the base of the PCF for more than twenty years',[25] at the same time as for his intellectual contributions.

Debray's wish to see 'no more divisions between professionals of the intelligence and professionals of political action – intellectuals and militants'[26] may seem excessively optimistic, in the light of the devaluation of political militancy in France since (broadly speaking) the election of François Mitterrand in 1981. I would argue, however, that his own involvement with the processes of political change, in Latin America and subsequently as Third World adviser to Mitterrand, along with the importance his later work, from *Le Pouvoir intellectuel en France* of 1979 onwards, attaches to the long-term systemic reasons for the decline in the importance of the political, both show that the relationship between the intellectual and political activity is almost as important a theme for Debray as it was for Sartre.

The trajectories of the two men are very different; Marxism for Sartre was the culmination of a long meditation on individual freedom and essence, catalysed by World War Two, whereas for Debray it was much more a philosophical and political starting-point. Yet an observation such as 'Everything which hinders the intellectual's personal commitment to the history of his age, a history made by the organised vanguards, side by side with all the workers, diminishes the area of his contact with life, reduces his creative capacity and delays the advent of socialism'[27] clearly evokes the Sartrean stress on the individual's inseparability from the history to which s/he is always answerable – a stress that (albeit in less ethically challenging form) will inform the whole of Debray's work.

Revolution in the Revolution? was first published in Cuba (300 000 copies!) and very shortly afterwards in France, Britain and the US in 1967; it thus owes much of its notoriety to Debray's imprisonment in that year. Sartre's observation that 'Régis Debray has been arrested by the Bolivian authorities, not for having participated in guerrilla activities, but for having written a book – *Revolution in the Revolution?*'[28] acquires an ironic dimension in the light of Sartre's own frequent, and unavailing, attempts to get himself arrested in Gaullist France, but there is little doubt that he was right. The work's non-biographical importance lay primarily in the fact that it suggested a third way towards revolutionary change, following neither the Russian nor the Chinese model, and thus to quote Leo Huberman and Paul M. Sweezy in their foreword that: 'if a third way is possible, then those of us who live in countries where conditions are basically different from those obtaining in Tsarist Russia or Kuomintang China or contemporary Latin America, had better ask ourselves very seriously whether still other revolutionary patterns may not be possible.'[29]

The breaking-up of the monolithic model of revolutionary change – one of the major political developments of the late 1960s – has continued apace ever since. Edgar Morin, in 1978, was to describe the very term 'revolution' as 'polluted',[30] following on revelations about not only the USSR but China, Kampuchea and even Debray's once beloved Cuba, and the term has now all but fallen into disuse on the European left, not least because the major revolutionary changes of recent years, in Eastern Europe, have led to the overthrow of self-styled Leninist states.

Revolution in the Revolution? may thus now appear as an ironic elegy to the idea of revolution rather than as its most stimulating embodiment, but once again it should be emphasised that this is true only from the Western perspective within which Debray's book has probably most often been read. Today's Latin America is a continent still subject to (literally) revolutionary change, in which the recent gains of democracy are still often precarious and notions of armed struggle anything but outmoded. Debray begins by stressing that 'the Latin American revolutionary war possesses highly special and profoundly distinct conditions of development, which can only be discovered through a particular experience'[31] – a formulation that condenses the stress on material particularity that is apparent throughout his work, evidenced in the high esteem in which he holds geography or the 'pre-linguistic' work of the paleontologist André Leroi-Gourhan.

It is on the grounds of these 'highly special and profoundly distinct conditions of existence' that Debray rejects on the one hand the view that armed self-defence of the masses is sufficient (it is dismissed as corresponding 'on the military level to the failure of reformism on the political level'),[32] on the other the Trotskyist extrapolation of 'a direct passage from union action to insurrection'.[33] Debray criticises Trotskyism in terms not dissimilar to those in which Henri Lefebvre criticised structuralism,[34] for its metaphysical immobilism and immutability ('In space – everywhere the same ... In time – immutable').[35] The Trotskyist analysis, for him, is quite literally lethal ('To promote public assemblies of the people in an Indian village, or open union meetings, is simply to denounce the inhabitants to the forces of repression and the political cadres to the police: it is to send them to prison or their graves').[36]

The alternative Debray counterposes to reformist self-defence and Trotskyist metaphysics is that of armed propaganda, carried out by small, flexible and tightly disciplined guerrilla patrols. This had worked well in the struggle against French rule in Vietnam in the 1940s, though for Debray Latin America's sparsity of population and firmly-established local repressive régimes mean that the military pyramid of liberation is likely to be built from the top down rather than from the base up. The extraordinarily difficult conditions under which the Latin American struggles took place meant that military action – as it were leading by example – was the most important form of revolutionary propaganda, and that the slogan 'Patria o Muerte!' needed, as Guevara discovered, to be taken with shocking literalness. To succumb to the temptation of mapping one overall strategy – Trotskyist, Chinese, Vietnamese or even Cuban – onto a host of different national situations is for Debray an occupational hazard for the intellectual, himself included:

> That an intellectual, especially if he is a bourgeois, should speak of strategy before all else, is normal. Unfortunately, however, the right road, the only feasible one, sets out from tactical data,

> rising gradually towards the definition of strategy. The abuse of strategy and the lack of tactics is a delightful vice, characteristic of the contemplative man – a vice to which we, by writing these lines, must plead guilty.[37]

Strategy – the grand sweep of overall design – is both more readily accessible to intellectuals in their armchairs or libraries and more congenial to their synthesising mode of thought than the messy, difficult, materially constricted business of tactics. This latter, however, must in the context in which Debray is working (about as far removed as possible from the accustomed surroundings of the Parisian intellectual) determine the course of action, even where this comes to seem impossibly isolated or precarious. 'In the initial stage [sc. of a guerrilla campaign] the base of support is in the guerrilla fighter's knapsack';[38] this evocation of Napoleon's 'An army marches on its stomach' emphasises how crucial to an effective struggle flexibility and mobility are. In this way 300 Cuban *guerrilleros* were able to rout 10,000 regular soldiers in 1958, not as the result of some medieval miracle of faith, but because of the military preparedness and determination of the combatants.

An orthodox Marxist or Communist argument (as in Mao's 'Put politics in command') would hold that military action must at all times be subordinate to and governed by the correct political line – a rerunning of the 'strategy/tactics' dichotomy referred to above. This, for Debray, is liable to lead to quite literally fatal military errors, traceable to the dependence of the countryside upon the city which we have already seen to be implicit in the Leninist theory of revolution. Anybody without first-hand experience of the *guerrillero*'s 'material effort involved in eating, sleeping, moving from one place to another – briefly, in surviving'[39] is simply unable to determine the tactics such groups should follow. Debray's own move from Paris to Havana and thence to the Bolivian countryside (albeit as observer rather than participant) becomes politically as well as existentially understandable in this context.

Debray's assertion that those who 'believe that revolutionary awareness and organisation must and can in every sense precede revolutionary action' are moved by 'the same naïve idealism that inspires those who are addicted to the electoral opium, for whom socialism will come on the day when one half plus one of the electorate vote for it'[40] may seem to read oddly from one who was later to be involved with that supreme peddler of 'electoral opium', François Mitterrand; but Debray has consistently maintained that the revolutionary or insurrectionary road to social change, the only one possible in Latin America, was neither necessary nor desirable in a developed bourgeois society such as France. That action can determine awareness and organisation is a view eminently compatible with Marx's dictum that 'it is not the consciousness of men that determines their being, but, on the contrary, their social being that determines their consciousness.'[41] It was, however, often difficult to reconcile Debray's privileging of the armed combat unit, however small, with the paramountcy of the (Communist) Party. Thus, for Huberman and Sweezy, *Revolution in the Revolution?* is

> not merely a sort of handbook of revolutionary tactics ... but also, and in our opinion more importantly, a negation of the whole doctrine of revolutionary legitimacy, which has been one of the key components of Communist orthodoxy ever since the Russian Revolution.[42]

The importance of Castro for Debray becomes clearer if we see him as the archetypal fusion of military and political leadership, the second growing in struggle out of the first. Cuba's *jusqu'auboutiste* loyalty to the USSR was, as earlier suggested, often largely motivated by economic self-interest; not long after the Cuban revolution had proclaimed itself socialist, in 1961, disillusionment began to set in with Moscow (which had other things to do with its time than fanning the Latin American revolutionary flame) and with the Latin American Communist parties that followed its lead. Debray's ringing endorsement of Castro's view

> that there is no revolution without a vanguard; that this vanguard is not necessarily the Marxist-Leninist party; and that those who want to make the revolution have the right and the duty to constitute themselves as a vanguard, independently of these parties[43]

thus marks an alignment against orthodox (Moscow-led) Communism, and in this context it is easier to see why, for all his reservations about Maoism and the occasional savagery of his strictures on Trotskyism, the 'New Lefts' that were emerging in Europe and the USA at this time so readily claimed him as one of theirs.

The revolution(s) in Latin America mark, for Debray, a radical break with the previous subordination of military instrumentality to political leadership, and thus a devaluation of the importance of the various national Communist parties. The key political lesson he draws is that:

> Under certain conditions, the political and the military are not separate, but form one organic whole, consisting of the people's army, whose nucleus is the guerrilla army. The vanguard party can exist in the form of the guerrilla *foco* itself. The guerrilla force is the party in embryo.[44]

This is less a rejection of Marxist-Leninist theory than a bold appropriation of it from the traditional Communist parties and thus from Moscow and Beijing alike. The guerrillas are the Leninist vanguard party on the march, dialectically fusing the military and the political with the indispensable help of the radio transmitter, which 'produces a qualitative change in the guerrilla movement'.[45]

The stress on how technologies of transmission necessarily modify what can be transmitted – the central preoccupation of Debray's most recent work – here helps to explain how the guerrilla movement can become the political vanguard, for it is the radio transmitter that will enable contact between the guerrillas and the population outside the zone of operations, and thus bring about 'the alliance between workers and peasants'[46] – thus, between the urban and the rural – necessary if socialism is to be achieved.

The task of the guerrilla group is not confined to armed struggle and propaganda. The liberated zones it organises can (as happened in Cuba) become 'counter-societies' or models for the future liberated state, laboratories for 'agrarian reform, peasant congresses, levying of taxes, revolutionary tribunals, the discipline of collective life'.[47] In societies with low levels of literacy and population density, where the holding of public meetings was a desperately hazardous enterprise, so apparently utopian (or even Arcadian) a vision came to seem not merely practicable, but the only concrete possibility. Insurrection is thus not a substitute for political activity, but the form such activity takes in the highly specific circumstances outlined by Debray. 'Events would seem to indicate the need to focus all efforts on the practical organisation of the armed struggle with a view to achieving unity on the basis of Marxist-Leninist principles';[48] it was the prioritisation of armed struggle that gave *Revolution in the Revolution?* its profoundly subversive cast, and enabled the Bolivian government and the CIA to take an exemplary revenge on its author.

His arrest, beating and mistreatment in custody, and the refusal to allow him to be represented by a non-Bolivian lawyer, led to an international outcry which, whilst it did not palliate the sentence passed on him, secured him comparatively favourable conditions of incarceration, including access to books and (after a brief hunger strike) permission to give interviews. His trial speech, 'I Regret That I Am Innocent', emphasises that he was not actively involved with the guerrilla movement (as the prosecution had asserted), but that he was for all that in entire agreement and solidarity with its actions:

> As a revolutionary (to the extent to which I can be called one), I feel and I declare myself jointly responsible for all the 'crimes' committed by all revolutionaries everywhere in the world, from the printing of leaflets to attacks on banks to obtain funds, from

> illegal meetings to the execution of torturers ... [T]he very fact that I am staying in the revolutionary ranks and that I continue to be convinced that armed struggle is the key to the liberation struggle, particularly in Bolivia, proves that I do not repent of these so-called crimes and that I am prepared to continue committing them. I ratify them, and, adhering to the moral and political concepts which have inspired them, I also inevitably accept whatever consequences may arise from my actions.[49]

Figures as diversely eminent as André Malraux, François Mauriac, Picasso, Graham Greene (who contacted the Pope) and Jean-Luc Godard were active in the campaign for Debray's release. On the British and more particularly American New Left, Debray's ideas were kept before the public through the medium of fraternal debate, notably in the pages of the *Monthly Review*. The editors of this, New Leftists Huberman and Sweezy, criticise him there for seeking to prescribe one revolutionary course for all Latin American societies. For Eqbal Ahmad in the same volume, he oversimplifies the passage from the personal and group example of the guerrillas to a revolutionary politics, thereby turning the *foco* into 'a tailor's fit for the American counter-insurgency program'.[50] Hartmut Ramon proffers broadly similar criticism whilst indirectly pointing to an influence on Debray little noted at the time (though the subject of a brief article by him in *New Left Review*, January–February 1970) – Antonio Gramsci, whose 'pessimism of the intellect, optimism of the will' is as if echoed in the manner in which Debray 'dilutes the objective conditions required by Lenin for beginning an insurrection in order to accommodate Guevara's *foco* theory, which accents subjective conditions'.[51] Althusser, writing to Debray on 1 March 1967, urges him to provide more detailed analysis of the historical conditions of existence of the guerrilla rather than taking these as a fact of nature, arguing that 'the "solution" you put forward derives its strength not from a positive demonstration of its qualities, but from the failure of all the others (and thus the demonstration of their negative character)'.[52]

Debray's 'Reply to my Critics' (one of the only two letters that reached his friends in the first two years of his captivity) emphasises that his intention in *Revolution in the Revolution?* was to study actually existing movements of armed struggle rather than to enunciate general laws for its development in Latin America, and at the same time questions whether one can 'purge objective studies of revolutionary phenomena of all normative commitments for the future'[53] – the ambivalence of Marxism as diagnosis and Marxism as prognosis that was to prove so crucial a factor in its 1980s' and 1990s' decline.

Debray's *Prison Writings* betoken an understandable questioning of his role as a Parisian intellectual – mistrustful of Sartre ('his outbursts had a warmth of which we were suspicious'),[54] and even more so of a theory he describes as 'a very lax kind of rigorousness; restricted to the written word, it left us free to do what we wished in every other sphere'.[55] The 'written word' was later, we shall see, to assume a different importance for Debray. In the same text ('In Settlement of All Accounts', first published in Cuba in 1967), Debray refers to his intellectual generation's 'total lack of history'[56] – an allusion to the anti-Hegelian and anti-historicist cast of Marxism (embodied above all by Althusser) predominant in 1960s' Paris. Debray's Latin American involvement clearly marked a massive return of what might be called the repressed of history, and along with it of the problematisation of time (something with which any prisoner must rapidly become familiar). In 'Time and Politics' (published in *Les Temps Modernes* of June 1970), he says that 'a time of crisis is simply ordinary time concentrated'[57] – in context a clear allusion to the May 1968 events on which he was to comment more extensively eight years later, but also a reflection on the necessarily problematic nature of historical crises, and thus on the no less problematic nature of history:

> Thus if there is a choice (and refusing to make one is itself a choice) one can only opt for what seems the lesser of two evils. Furthermore it is not a deduction, but a gamble, in other words a well-judged leap in the dark.[58]

In this vocabulary, with its stress on history as action and on the concomitant need for the taking of risks not only in guerrilla combat, but in the more prosaic business of political alliance-forming and the devising of strategy, there can be detected a link between Debray's 'revolutionary period' in Latin America and his later work as an ally of Mitterrand's in France. Differing historical and institutional circumstances require differing tactics and strategies, and Debray has always been quite emphatic that his support for revolution in Latin America was in no way incompatible with his belief that in the constitutional republic of France, the electoral rather than the insurrectionary route to change was the only viable one. His clearest statement of this position came in a 1973 interview which merits extended quotation:

> There is no *continuity* between my activities ... in Latin America and my political positions in France, for the simple reason that in politics 'everything depends on conditions' (Lenin), and there is neither homogeneity nor continuity between historical conditions in Latin America (and the twenty-plus very dissimilar nations that make it up) and those in today's France ... I would

> not be a Marxist, a Leninist, a Guevarist, or anything else if I thought that the electoral route is the Bolivian people's best chance of political power; and I would not be a Marxist, a Leninist, a Guevarist, or anything else if I thought that revolutionary war was on the agenda in France.[59]

It thus seems imprecise to speak of Debray's 'revolutionary' and 'reformist' periods, since the distinction is as much one of culture and geography. His *Entretiens avec Allende sur la situation au Chili/Conversations with Allende on the Situation in Chile* (1971 – very soon after Allende had come to power) opens with an introduction in which he takes the régime fraternally to task for its supposedly obsessive legalism, and chillingly prefigures its eventual downfall ('Will what made it possible to govern [i.e. the bourgeois electoral system] not also be what makes it impossible to take power?').[60] The conversations themselves are a fairly classic dialogue between two exponents of the idea of revolution, one suspicious of constitutionalism (Debray is sceptical of the notion of 'proletarian legality'),[61] one defining that idea in terms that accommodate readily to the electoralist strategy that most European Communist parties were in the process of adopting ('[sc. revolution is] the shift of power from a minority to a majority class').[62]

The two volumes of *La Critique des armes* – translatable into English either as *Armed Criticism* or as *A Criticism of Arms* – prolong and continue Debray's preoccupation with the national specificity of revolutionary processes in Latin America. The first (called *La Critique des armes* – 1974) argues that 'Latin-American solidarity' is not achievable by an act of will, but requires to be anchored in the specificity – at once mythical and effective – of each participant nation:

> No politics achieves historical status if it does not include the realm of feeling, for the masses who make history do not set themselves going if their will is not stirred by a fundamental emotion or image anchored in the depths of their past history.[63]

The vocabulary of that last clause in particular may send shivers down more than a few spines, reminiscent as it is of a political irrationalism whose most spectacularly foul excrescences represent everything against which Debray and those before him fought. No 'irrationalism', however, is ever merely that, and the notion of myth, like that of ideology an inescapable component part of modern political discourse, is perhaps identifiable by its straddling or synthesis of the 'rational' and the 'irrational' – *mutatis mutandis* of the conscious and the unconscious. That of the nation – gloriously self-liberating for a Western leftist audience in Cuba or archetypally Vietnam, something horrendously different in 1930s' Germany or Italy – is doubtless the clearest exemplar of this.

That is further suggested by the companion volume to *La Critique des armes*, *La Guerrilla du Che/Che's Guerrilla Campaign* (1974), which situates in a specifically Bolivian context the Guevarist myth to whose continuing efficacy it nevertheless attests ('Che each day survives a little more his last adventure, as if he were himself even greater than this failed project, to which he yet gave the whole of himself').[64] Another productive way of understanding the importance of myth in the context of Debray's Latin American work is as the major point of intersection, dialogue or dialectic between the political and the literary. In this light, it is doubtless not accidental that Debray's two full-length novels – *L'Indésirable* of 1975 (English translation *Prohibited Immigrant*) and *La Neige brûle/The Snow is Burning* of 1977 – are both at least partially set in Latin America.

L'Indésirable centres on a European intellectual, Frank, working with guerrillas in an unnamed Latin American country, which the context plainly indicates to be Venezuela. Frank, 'who has set out to fuse with History in America, discovers as the struggle goes on the weight of the European soul' (according to the French jacket-note) – a reinscription of the importance of the geographical and the national as well as a fairly clear allusion to Debray's own relation with the continent. The novel closely interweaves political struggle with a love affair symptomatic of or caught up in that struggle (in which it is reminiscent of, in different ways, Hemingway's *A Farewell to Arms*, Malraux's *La Condition humaine*, or Sartre's *Les Chemins de la liberté*). Frank's affair is with Célia – the companion of the guerrilla leader Joaquim, imprisoned when the action of the novel begins – who sleeps with the Italian ex-Fascist agent Rossi to secure a shipment of arms. The killing of a number of guerrillas in the jungle convinces the leadership that the armed struggle is too risky an undertaking and that electoral alliances are a more viable way forward (an oblique reference to Allende?). Frank rejects this strategy, less in the name of the grand insurrectionary design than because:

> ... he is a man alone and one can be realistic only on one's home ground ... It was nothing but an image that guided him towards this land, a Pole Star that gives him courage when exile is too heavy to bear. If he betrays this image, he will not thereby rediscover American reality – that *terra incognita*, antipathetic to every fibre of his being – and he will undoubtedly lose any sense of direction.[65]

An ideological homeland alone not being enough, Frank shoots dead Rossi – political coinciding with sexual revenge – before himself being gunned down by the police. The kind of literary tradition in which I have attempted briefly to situate this novel now seems all but dead in a world in which heroic armed struggles are at a distinct premium, and the strenuously heady sensuality of the Great Political Romance with Célia ('give me your downy thighs to bite in the morning, the fuselage of your legs without promise of tomorrow')[66] is likely to arouse laughter at best. Where *L'Indésirable* remains of more than museum-piece interest, however, is in its articulation of the relationship – confused, often contradictory – between the national and the international. It is no coincidence that Frank is a Trotskyist – thus, an adherent of the Marxist tradition most uncompromisingly committed to international struggle. Yet in Venezuela he discovers that internationalism is a matter of difference and of barriers as much, and at the same time, as of solidarity and shared revolutionary programmes. 'Bolivar is using Marx for a posthumous triumph'[67] – an allusion to the at least chronological primacy of the national struggles in Latin America, and one that justifies (or rationalises) Frank's (and/or Debray's) sense that in a very fundamental way he will always be foreign to those struggles.

This is not to make of *L'Indésirable* a reactionary text of defeat. To quote the jacket once more, 'whilst it may appear a lonely one, [Frank's] sacrifice draws its meaning from the fact that it keeps alive this kind of fidelity' – that between fighters in the same cause of which Debray had first-hand experience in Latin America. That the novel's only significant *femme* is conspicuously *fatale* will come as no surprise if one has the slightest knowledge of *macho* revolutionary politics – especially in Latin America – of the time; but Célia is also very much 'a woman in her own right', clearer and less tormented in her revolutionary commitment than the deracinated Frank and able to run side by side with enviable equanimity her affair with Frank, her *liaison de convenance* with Rossi and her never-seriously-challenged *grand amour* with Joaquim.

Debray's second (and to date last) novel, *La Neige brûle*, won the Prix Fémina (awarded by an all-woman jury) in 1977. The triangle of narrative protagonist (Boris), guerrilla leader (Carlos), and woman committed to the revolution (Imilla) remains from *L'Indésirable*, but with the significant difference that Boris's relationship with Imilla remains platonic throughout. After she has shot dead a former Bolivian police chief (now Consul in Hamburg) Boris desires her even more, but by that time she is on her way back to certain death in Bolivia, having 'chosen to call love what already connects her to the infinite line of comrades who have fallen'.[68] Imilla resembles Célia in the autonomy she exercises in her choice of lovers side by side with a fundamental monogamy; when she is in love with and pregnant by Carlos (and still busy smuggling arms), 'the woman no longer had to play a double game with the militant ... in becoming one man's woman, she finally felt fully herself'.[69]

More relevant from our point of view than these splendid extravagances are the fundamental Debray themes that recur in this text – the vast difference between European and Latin American societies, and consequently of appropriate modes of political struggle (Boris to the half-Austrian Imilla: 'In Europe there are civilised police-forces, with lawyers, law-courts, examining magistrates, and special status for political prisoners')[70] and the dramatic, irrevocable and thereby fascinating nature of violence, distilled in a memorable passage:

> Since the world has existed, it has taken nine months to make a child, two years for a resistance network, ten years for a political party and thirty for a revolution. Since the world has existed, it has taken no more than one second to kill a human being, a minute to destroy a network, a day to sabotage a revolution.[71]

The dynamic of *La Neige brûle*, as of all Debray's Latin American work, resides in the interaction of the two time-scales – one might almost speak of orders of temporality – mentioned here, and his later stress on armament and defence is perhaps to be traced back to his first-hand experience of the time-scales described (thirty years, we should remember, was the length of the prison sentence passed on him) as much as to the more specifically French context with which we shall deal in the next chapter. That context makes its appearance in the narration when, after Carlos's death, Imilla comes to stay with Boris in Paris, where she is gratified to encounter the women's movement – the only successful revolution inasmuch as it is not 'programmed, organised or even foreseen by any card-carrying revolutionary'.[72] Debray also provides himself in this section with a good excuse to vent his spleen against those Parisian intellectuals who, in the wake of Solzhenitsyn's revelations about the Gulag Archipelago and the failure of revolutionary political options to make a real mark in Europe, had abandoned their erstwhile commitment for the ersatz spirituality of the 'new philosophy' ('Finished eh revolution socialism old myths Marx is dead old friend the old illusions have gone pop exit out now it's the new buzz of transcendence').[73] The self-consciously avant-garde (absence of) punctuation is clearly designed to evoke the novelist and literary theoretician Philippe Sollers, among the leaders of the 'retreat from Marx', while the 'new buzz of transcendence' is no less clearly reminiscent of 'new philosophers' such as Bernard-Henri Lévy.[74] Imilla's response ('So it's for all this shit that you dropped us?')[75] is all the more understandable given that Debray had had to renegotiate his relationship to the left in considerably less congenial circumstances than those of the Rive Gauche world he lampoons.

La Neige brûle is unquestionably a finer piece of work than *L'Indésirable* – more assured, more complex in its frame of reference, more multi-layered in the ironies of its rendezvous between European and Latin American histories and sensibilities. Latin America was not to disappear from Debray's life or work for good; his imprisonment is revisited in the aphoristic *Journal d'un petit bourgeois entre deux feux et quatre murs/The Diary of a Petit-Bourgeois Caught in the Middle and Between Four Walls* of 1976. From now on, however, as a European living in Europe, and more particularly a French intellectual living – the statement is almost tautologous – in Paris, his preoccupations were to be less geographically far-flung, though as we shall also see in their own way scarcely less exotic. 'You no longer have a father because you know now that you will remain basically a little boy, and that all the fathers in the world will not change that.'[76] The existential self-searching epitomised in that sentence was to recur powerfully in *Les Masques* and, along with the cauterising analytical gaze Debray was to turn upon the milieu to which he had just returned, to provide the major impetus for his work in the following years.

CHAPTER 2

The 'French Debray': Politics, Intellectuals and the Media in France

Debray returned to France, as he relates in *Les Masques*,[77] in the spring of 1971, after two months spent in Havana, to live in a flat belonging to Yves Montand and Simone Signoret on the Ile de la Cité, right in the centre of Paris. The multiplicity of the cultural shock will be apparent from this brief description, reinforced by his growing apartness from Élisabeth Burgos, whom he had married whilst in prison and with whom he was shortly nevertheless to have a daughter ... 'May 68 and women's liberation, of which I knew nothing, had meanwhile been along.'[78] Both these movements, in different ways, were to find a place in Debray's later work. In the meantime, it is scarcely surprising that four years passed before he published a new text.

This – *Les Rendez-Vous Manqués/Missed Appointments* of 1975 – was written for, and dedicated to, the French Castroist militant Pierre Goldman, who had just been wrongfully imprisoned for the murder of a chemist whose shop he was allegedly trying to rob. (Goldman was finally to be acquitted in 1978, only to be murdered in still-unexplained circumstances in 1979) *Les Rendez-Vous Manqués* is, unsurprisingly, a burning call for justice, but also the first text in which Debray articulates what were to be the major themes of his work for some time. The Mitterrand of the 1960s is described as 'the future, arriving too late in a world that was too new',[79] whilst the verbosity of May 1968 and its aftermath is seen as having had results diametrically opposed to what might have been expected at the time ('The great festival of the leftist intelligentsia in fact marked the moment when the right took power within the intelligentsia').[80]

The Marxist intellectual hegemony that had prevailed in France since the Liberation was, with the rise of the 'new philosophers' – notably André Glucksmann and Bernard-Henri Lévy – and their humanist spirituality in response to Solzhenitsyn's revelations about the Gulag and the no less dreadful tidings from China and Cambodia/Kampuchea, in the process of being overturned.[81] That loss of intellectual power was soon to be accompanied, with the right's unexpected victory in the 1978 parliamentary elections, by political defeat.

François Mitterrand's no less unexpected presidential triumph in 1981 turned out, paradoxically, to mark a further setback for the Marxist left, for the Parti Socialiste then and thenceforth comprehensively outflanked its Communist *frère ennemi*. Debray's impassioned call to action ('We must save a man, a comrade. Pierre Goldman is you and I')[82] is at the same time a recognition of which way the political wind was to blow in a France where 'the bourgeoisie disgusts us and the great day has been and gone: what is to be done?'.[83]

The 1978 electoral defeat was particularly galling for the French left, coming as it did ten years after those May 1968 events that had seemed to promise so much. *Modeste contribution aux discours et cérémonies officielles du dixième anniversaire/A Modest Contribution to the Discourses and Official Ceremonies of the Tenth Anniversary* is Debray's attempt to deal with those events and the change they portended, differing from most other such attempts up till then in its assertion that 'May 68 is the cradle of the new bourgeois society.'[84] This view rests on the disparity (for Debray at its maximum immediately before May) between France's technological and industrial development since 1945 and its comparative social and structural stagnation:

> French society, which had become 'anti-economic(al)', was in the long term compromising the viability of 'France plc'. The time came for the first to catch up with the second, and it was so far behind that double helpings were needed. In this bringing up to date of 'Daddy's France', we felt a gust of madness, which was only the economy giving a common-sense lesson to society, the enforced submission of the old to the new.[85]

It requires some effort of recontextualisation to appreciate the effect this analysis must have produced at the time – one year before the election of Thatcher and three before that of Mitterrand, who can be seen as epitomising respectively 'the economy giving a common-sense lesson to society' and the 'bringing up to date [via a social-democratic process of modernisation] "Daddy's France"' (which thus became that of 'Tonton'/'Uncle' – Mitterrand's nickname from the time of the first period of cohabitation). The fact that Debray had spent May 1968 in a Latin American cell rather than on a Latin Quarter barricade doubtless combined with the 1978 disillusionment of the left to ensure a respectful reception for his text. Subsequent texts drawing on and articulating superficially similar themes in a less radical, more postmodernist way (Gilles Lipovetsky's *L'Ere du vide*, for example, which all but voids the events of any substantive social content by viewing them as the herald of the 'me generations' of the late 1970s and early 1980s)[86] have tended to blunt the radicalism of an analysis for which 'the overthrow of the capitalist system remains the only wager compatible with our dignity, and it is not an unreasonable one'.[87]

The impulse of 1968 was certainly a modernising one, articulated in the anti-de Gaulle chant of 'Ten years is enough!' and the extravagant reaction against the obscurantist and mandarin culture of the old Sorbonne. The plurality of individualities, subjectivities, expressions that the events demanded, and to which they gave rise, was enabled and diffused by that same incipient media age that ensured their containment within, or neutralisation by, late capitalist society. May 1968 thus marked the point at which 'the discourse-event – or anything at all – became *something* by virtue of its reproduction in the media'.[88]

With the prescience of this analysis – one year before Norman Mailer's *Miami and the Siege of Chicago* – it is difficult to disagree. It is (largely) without irony that Debray proclaims 'far from me the idea of encroaching on the ritual consecration of May ("the greatest adventure of a generation")'.[89] Beyond this consecration and what it represented, however, what Debray signals here is recognisable as the threat of a depoliticised postmodernism – that for which no operative (as against theoretical) distinction exists between event and representation. *Modeste contribution* warns against such a collapsing, complicity with which was left to Lipovetsky and its other epigones.

Debray's *Lettre aux communistes français et à quelques autres/Letter to the French Communists and Some Others* (also 1978) is in many ways a complement or companion-piece to *Modeste contribution*. It was written before the 1978 elections, whose consequences for the Communists it ironically predicts:

> After the coming elections, which will see 'the irresistible rise of progressive forces' (under way by definition, and especially if we fail), we shall therefore go down into the street *en masse* to capture words as compensation for the Bastille and to present a student rag as a form of revenge.[90]

The 'student rag' in question clearly refers to May 1968, much as the reference to words and the Bastille evokes Michel de Certeau's analysis of the linguistic importance of May, *La prise de parole/The Capture of the Word*, which begins: 'In May we captured the word as the Bastille was captured in 1789.'[91]

The 'irresistible rise of progressive forces', conversely, formed part of the PCF's stock-in-trade of the 1970s – the period of 'Eurocommunism' and of 'broad anti-monopolist alliances' – so that the linguistic montage Debray effects here highlights the fundamental, and ultimately all but fatal, contradiction of the Party at the time, between revolutionary rhetoric and electoral practice. The PCF, of course, was even less disposed to 'go down into the street *en masse*' in 1978 than it had been ten years previously, and its entanglement in its own contradictions was to make of it, in Debray's terms:

> ... a party whose fundamental goal was not to build socialism, but to rebuild itself over and over again, and whose aim was not to make France the leading socialist country in the world, but to remain itself the leading political party in France.[92]

The PCF having achieved none of the four goals listed other than its own reconstruction on an ever smaller scale, alignment with the 'bourgeois-democratic' Parti Socialiste came to seem the only viable option on the left ('On one hand, the diversions of revisionism; on the other, the certainty of remaining at a standstill').[93] Debray's later involvement with François Mitterrand (for whom he worked as adviser on Third World affairs from 1981 to 1985 and from 1987 to 1988) thus represents a 'break', or in more judgemental terms a 'betrayal', only on either an extremely superficial or a highly sectarian reading.

Significant as all this may be, it does not of itself make Debray's 'French' career sufficiently important to justify a monograph such as the present one. That career has been marked by a growing preoccupation with the varying modes of mediation by which a social formation represents itself, and thus with changing types of communication (above all the shift from printed word to visual image).

Such mediations are necessary, in something very like an ultimate philosophical or even anthropological sense, because of the necessary *incompleteness* of human social organisation – for Debray the linchpin of his life's intellectual endeavours. Recent French thought has foregrounded the illusory, provisional – precisely, incomplete – nature of what it had been customary to regard as in some sense self-contained linguistic, social, textual or psychological systems; the work of Roland Barthes, Jacques Derrida, Michel Foucault, Jacques Lacan in different ways bears witness to this. Debray's work inscribes itself within a very different (set of) context(s) – nobody has ever called him, however misguidedly, a 'structuralist', few would think of him as a theoretical guru – yet the centrality of incompleteness to his work seems to me in many respects to partake of a similar conceptual repertory to that of the thinkers just mentioned.

The most concise and lucid account of this notion is to be found in the transcribed radio interviews with the Swiss sociologist and Third World specialist Jean Ziegler, *Il s'agit de ne pas se rendre/The Important Thing is not to Surrender*, in which Debray adapts the theorem of the mathematician Gödel to a socio-anthropological context:

> No group can close itself using only elements immanent to itself. This means that there will always be irrationality in any human society. A group exists only through its closure, and one cannot close oneself without at the same time opening onto or referring to something transcendental – the founding hero, the lost paradise, the Last Judgement, the universal republic, the classless society, or whatever.[94]

The first text in which Debray begins to develop this fundamental concept of his later thought is *Le Scribe/The Scribe* of 1980, but what might be termed the transition from polemical intervention in contemporary affairs to a wider-ranging philosophical reflection – the opposite path to that travelled by Sartre – had in fact begun a year earlier, with *Le Pouvoir intellectuel en France/Intellectual Power in France* (translated into English as *Writers, Critics, Celebrities*).

The founding thesis of this work is comparatively simple – that 'the integration with the major channels of diffusion through which the upper intelligentsia has bought its social supremacy has been paid for by a marked degradation of the intellectual function'.[95] The changing role of the French intellectual in a culture far less verbal, less politically committed, and more visual than heretofore was, especially after Sartre's death in 1980, to command increasing attention. It is scarcely an accident that the throne Sartre (however unwillingly) occupied has since remained vacant. Not only have the most influential serious writers in France tended to come from the field of the human sciences as much as from that of literature (Barthes has almost certainly been as widely read and studied as the Robbe-Grillet he was instrumental in bringing to public notice), but the role of writing itself, as elsewhere in the West, has been less and less culturally central.

Not so, however, that of the writer; and it is against this divorce between producer and text, and even more between the production of written texts and their diffusion, that Debray inveighs. Debray's major institutional target is what was then the most popular 'intellectual' French television programme – *Apostrophes*, presented by Bernard Pivot, who each Friday evening interviewed the authors of a number of the week's most important new books. It is difficult to imagine such a programme becoming a beloved national institution in Britain or the USA, but the immense popularity of *Apostrophes* ensured considerable, and by no means always favourable, attention for *Le Pouvoir intellectuel en France*. Debray turned down a predictable invitation to appear on the programme (though he was to do so in 1986, pleading weariness of 'playing the anti-Pivot'), and was the centre of a major dispute in 1981 when on a visit to Montreal he attacked Pivot's 'dictatorship' over French intellectual life in an interview. Debray claimed that whilst on an official mission of state he had spoken (albeit injudiciously) as a private citizen, and the affair, like most of its kind, duly blew over.

Much more significant in the long term than Debray's tilting at the immense symbolic power undoubtedly exercised by one man, however, is the pungency and prescience of his analysis, at once historical and structural, of the distribution of symbolic power across changing institutional sites. The 'three ages' Debray identifies are the university cycle (1880–1930), the publishing cycle (1920–1960) and the media cycle (from 1968 to the present). As first the universities, then the world of publishing, expanded, it became increasingly difficult for individuals within those spheres to maintain their influence, for 'the power of an élite is in inverse proportion to its number'.[96] The chronological overlap between the three ages suggests that they are not entirely distinct, for the characteristic configuration Debray describes is one where the same individual works at once as academic, as series editor and as journalist. Such a concentration of power within an inevitably restricted circle of individuals no less inevitably leads to the hegemony of the media, with their higher 'social visibility'[97] and increasing capacity to dictate the terms of cultural and intellectual success.

This makes the aforementioned divorce between production and diffusion – more and more characteristic for Debray of the 'upper intelligentsia' in particular – much easier to understand. An individual whose time is divided between teaching and examining theses, commissioning and vetting manuscripts and reviewing other people's work is likely to have comparatively little time for serious productive research of his/her own, whence the dominance of the broker, the publicist, the diffuser in the 'upper intelligentsia'. Whence, too, that intelligentsia's increasing gravitation away from the institutions of the state towards those of the free market – for Debray, as a man of the left and a lifelong believer in the nation state, a movement that can only be deplored. The 'lower intelligentsia' – those who carry out the subaltern tasks of teaching, research, publication – are on the contrary likely to 'want the state because it is by it that they live'[98] (especially bearing in mind the effective state monopoly of education in France). To the objection that one type of intellectual production complements rather than competes with another ('it takes all sorts to make a world'), Debray retorts that there are '*limits to the elasticity of demand*', and that the 'world' in question here is one 'where each best-seller stands upon the lifeless body of a host of unsold texts (or "worst-sellers")'.[99]

What Debray describes is structurally at any rate not a new phenomenon. The Balzac of *Illusions perdues/Lost Illusions*, admiringly evoked in Debray's introduction ('Honoré de Balzac is the founding father of mediology ... Let nobody enter here who is not a Balzacian'),[100] had all but a century and a half before savagely anatomised the coteries and clientelism already characteristic of the nascent literary Paris of his day. It is the 'silence of intellectuals about the intelligentsia'[101] – bad faith and wanton narcissism forming an unholy alliance – that Debray most severely criticises. This was not to be a long-lasting phenomenon. The sociologist Pierre Bourdieu in much of his work (notably *Homo Academicus* of 1984) was to analyse the social and institutional distribution of the French intelligentsia, and on a more anecdotal – even journalistic – level Hervé Hamon and Patrick Rotman in *Les Intellocrates/The Intellocrats* and François de Negroni in *Le Savoir-Vivre intellectuel* were shortly to gratify their audience's (doubtless vicarious) narcissism with succulent anecdotes about which Left Bank brasseries were frequented by which publishing houses or about the sexual and alcoholic propensities of X or Y.

Nor, more sombrely, have the phenomena Debray describes turned out to have a purely local – geographically or chronologically restricted – existence. It is tempting for a British or American audience to ascribe them, with a gesture of envious dismissal, to the crushing centralisation of French cultural life on Paris ('Telephone directories list 337 bookstores in Chicago, 455 in New York, 456 in London, and 1239 in Paris').[102] That makes of Paris, however, less an exception than a microcosm – of that contemporary West that 'lives in a state of symbolic famine and of cultural force-feeding'.[103] The fifteen years since Debray's book appeared have given those words increased strength and pertinence, with the end of the Cold War and consequent disappearance of the old bipolar certainties as with the resistible rise of postmodernism and concomitant plurality of images raucously refusing to symbolise anything other than themselves.

The problem posed by *Le Pouvoir intellectuel en France*, as by many another analysis of contemporary societies, is what (if anything) can be done to remedy the situation it describes. Any discursive criticism of the media, Debray points out in the book's final paragraphs, is caught in a trap, for the very objects of that criticism can simply choose to ignore it. Principled individual withdrawal from the whole grimy fray is of limited use, for 'a historical and collective question can have only a historical and collective solution';[104] yet what that solution might be, short of the revolutionary overthrow of capitalist society, is far from clear in the text. *Le Pouvoir intellectuel en France* on its appearance was the object not of a conspiracy of silence so much as of what Herbert Marcuse refers to as 'recuperation' – absorbed itself into the system it denounced, becoming an effective part of it through its very rejection (as with the invitation to Debray to appear on *Apostrophes* – an elementary but classic 'Catch 22'). Certain of the cultural policies introduced by the Socialist government in 1981, notably the imposition of a minimum retail price for books, can be seen as a response to Debray's criticisms of the 'massification' of literary culture (in which 'in a society where the circulation of goods governs communication between human beings, the speed of stock turnover determines that of types and fashions of thought').[105] Yet in the interval the structural phenomena Debray describes have remained as pervasive as ever, and if the breathless modishness he evokes is no longer so apparent, that has to do with the stagnancy of French intellectual life at the time of writing (1995) rather than with any longer-term systemic change.

This pays an ironic tribute to the enduring force of the text's analyses, which rest in the last resort on the shift from a culture of the word – spoken, written or printed – to one of the image, but also on the absolute necessity for any form of social organisation to generate discourses that justify its legitimacy. (The names of Gramsci and Habermas may provide useful reference-points here.) This notion provides a bridge between *Le Pouvoir intellectuel* and *Le Scribe*, best demonstrated by a juxtaposition of the jacket-notes for each:

> The intellectuals have not betrayed. They do their job as statesmen better and better. In the West, the policing of minds has become a public service. It is because order reigns in people's brains that it reigns in the street. (*Le Pouvoir intellectuel*)

> Intellectuals never betray. When they mind what is not their own business – public affairs – they lay bare the most intimate truth of the political. To follow through, from the scribe of early days to the intellectual of today, the individual whose task it is to articulate the legitimacy or illegitimacy of power is to take the royal road to the sanctuary of any public life ... There is a bizarre 'affinity' between the mysteries of politics and those of religion, which needed to be demonstrated. (*Le Scribe*)

The references to intellectual betrayal will be readily perceived by a French audience as allusions to Julien Benda's *La Trahison des clercs/The Betrayal of the Intelligentsia* – a text written in 1927 as a polemic against those intellectuals willing to turn a blind eye to abuses of power and thereby compromise their truth-telling mission. (Benda, a Jewish socialist, had been a strong supporter of Dreyfus, which had cost him the coveted literary Prix Goncourt in 1912 – 'intellectual power in France' in action ....) The intellectual's search for abiding or transcendental truth stands in an evident tension with his/her necessarily public – hence, *a priori*, in some sense committed – role. The centrality of the intellectual in French life – from the Enlightenment harbingers of the Revolution through the Dreyfus affair (at which time the term 'intellectual' was originally coined by the anti-Dreyfusard Maurice Barrès as a pejorative term) to the Sartrean stress on commitment – means that in Paris more than anywhere else this tension has been acutely felt.[106] Paris, for Debray, represents metonymically the whole not merely of Western, but of written culture, and the transition from *Le Pouvoir intellectuel* to *Le Scribe* can thus be understood as an extrapolation of the more limited, tactical, pamphleteering approach of the earlier work onto a wider-ranging, more strategic and analytic level. It should be borne in mind that Debray was shortly to begin working for the newly-elected President Mitterrand, and that the Sartre who sold the banned Maoist newspaper *La Cause du Peuple* in the street, indefatigably signed petitions, and took part in demonstrations, was at the same time writing his dauntingly dense study of Flaubert (*L'Idiot de la famille/The Idiot of the Family*). Therefore the over-simplification of any view of this shift as a simple retreat from commitment back into the academy, tempting in the light of Debray's later career as it may be, should not be too hard to see.

Le Scribe's first section is entitled, in a clear reference to the work of Michel Foucault, 'The Genealogy of Power', and traces the role of the intellectual from the Holy Roman Empire through to contemporary France, asserting that '*the function of reference to the absolute*, or clerical function, is an invariable in any society'.[107] So bold and totalising a sweep is readily recognisable as 'French', and the third chapter of this section – 'The man [sic] among all men, or the French example' – traces the particular prominence of intellectuality in French national life back to 1789 and the universalising discursive claims of the Revolution:

> France did not, to be sure, invent human rights – either the idea, explored by all European theoreticians of natural law, or the legal formulation, whose first official version was the English Bill of Rights of 1688. But this determined only the civil liberties of subjects of the Crown. The Declaration of 26 August 1789 does not proclaim the rights of the French, but those of men and citizens. It is at one and the same time – and this is why it is a historic moment – universal and political, the 'and' corresponding at least implicitly to an equals sign.[108]

If this comes perilously close to staking out French territorial rights over the invention of humanity, it by the same token provides an explanation at once historical and structural – which is to say exempt from (the crasser kinds of) national generalisations – for the centrality of universal themes in French intellectual and political life, from Rousseau's human nature 'free but everywhere in chains' through to Foucault or Althusser, for whom in different ways 'man' or 'humanity' was a chimera. The distinctiveness of Debray's thought in this section lies less in its recognition that 'the organic link of culture with institutions is a political fact, not a social one'[109] – something of a self-evidence for the Marxist tradition at any rate – than in its assertion that the role of the 'clerk/cleric' or 'scribe' is an immutable given in any social formation. The very word '*clerc*' in French evokes not an office drudge or pen-pusher but, precisely, a member of the (actual or symbolic) clergy, and the political for Debray thus partakes structurally of the religious:

> Since no social formation – including a communist society, supposing such a thing to be possible – is conceivable unless its members have an imaginary relationship to their real conditions of existence, and since this relationship entails the legal and material setting-up of specialised institutions, there will always be a need for ideologues – the priesthood or the lay intelligentsia [*clergé* in French – translator].[110]

The reference to 'an imaginary relationship to their real conditions of existence' evokes Althusser's work on ideology, which he saw not as a veiling or distortion of that true scientific knowledge Marxism alone could vouchsafe but, following Lacan, as a necessary constitutive part of individuals' perception of themselves and their society. Debray's claims, however, go beyond those of Marxism (at the time he was writing still aspiring to hegemony), or for that matter any ideology at all, to posit something like a theorem – structural, conceptual, spiritual, or all three – that 'a group that has only its own elements to define itself will never become a totality'.[111] This is the first major appearance of the theme of incompleteness already referred to, a theme whose status is best understood as heuristic – 'something like a theorem' but not actually one, for Debray himself an intuition by its very nature not falsifiable, and thus unable to lay claim to 'truth' in the sense in which Karl Popper uses the term in *The Poverty of Historicism*. Given that such a claim would presumably be able to justify itself only within, precisely, a closed or complete system, it is hard to see how this could have been otherwise. (There is a potentially interesting parallel with the Derridean notion of difference/differance, notably in *Writing and Difference*, and its view of any textual closure as necessarily provisional and temporary.)

The Debray who wrote 'A state needs discourses to perpetuate itself as much as its enemies do to overthrow it'[112] had already produced a variety of discourses aiming to overthrow states in Latin America and to perpetuate the Fifth Republic (albeit with a socialist inflection) in France. He was writing, that is to say, in the tradition of the French 'public writer' defined by Priscilla Parkhurst Clark ('The twentieth-century public writer is the intellectual, a very different creature from the philosophe and the prophet, though clearly of the same lineage').[113] That lineage, for Debray, is not (only) a French one; it is common to any social formation.

The second section of *Le Scribe* begins with an interrogation of the role of intellectuals in Marx's thought. This is not the same as the role of Marxism for intellectuals, which as we have seen was dominant from the end of World War Two through to about the time at which Debray was writing. In the chapter entitled 'Marxist idealism, or Marx against intellectuals', Debray argues that for Marx intellectuals 'have no ... autonomous existence or specific function. They appear only as the "political and literary representatives" of social classes, which are the only real subjects of the movement.'[114] One corollary of this is that Marxist intellectuals have given little or no place to the structures and organisations – the mediations – by which Marxism has been reproduced and diffused. Debray's 'myriad of intellectuals measuring their scientific distinction by the distance that separates them from the Vulgate'[115] is a phrase that could have come from Bourdieu's *Distinction* (published the previous year), which uncharitably but pointedly ascribes intellectuals' preoccupation with textual purity to a desire to maintain their distinguished distance from the vulgar business of engagement with society. In both Debray and Bourdieu we are witness to in Freudian terms a return of that repressed that gave the intelligentsia, above all in France, its particularly *closed* quality. That adjective refers less (for Debray at all events) to its social or textual hermeticism than to the self-sufficient system that intellectual Marxism had become. '"Marxism is all-powerful because it is true"'; this dictum of Lenin's (which became the epigraph for the heavily Althusser-influenced *Cahiers marxistes-léninistes*, published at the École Normale Supérieure during Debray's time there) 'makes the concrete history of Marxism perfectly inexplicable'.[116] Marx's own reluctance to ascribe a specific status to the intellectual – a status assumed in a Leninist perspective by the revolutionary party, whose mediating role closes where that of the intellectual is to open – is seen as diminishing rather than increasing the prospect of social change. This somewhat surprising conclusion becomes less so if we reflect that for Debray the intellectual's role is above all that of mediator (as priests mediated God to humanity), and that without mediation any effective politics is inconceivable. '*If Marx had been right, Marxism would not exist.* Communist ideas would have been born of their own accord, out of factory life, and the expansion of industry would have been enough to organise the workers.'[117]

Intellectuals of the right are no more indulgently treated. From immediately after World War One through the 1935 'intellectuals' manifesto' opposing sanctions against Italy for the invasion of

Abyssinia, and thence to the 1978 'Manifesto of the intellectuals' committee for a free Europe' – by which is clearly meant a white nationalist/individualist Europe – the equation is immutable. 'Intellectuals = Intelligence = France or Europe = the Human Race or Essence.'[118] What is forgotten, in the pseudo-metaphysical self-importance and complacent narcissistic closure of this formula, is the literal material cost it entails. The 'white man's burden' of the intellectual life is as much an illusion as its colonial counterpart. Debray reminds us, in accents reminiscent of that Sartre who ate and drank daily at Les Deux Magots but knew who was paying the price, that:

> In a planet with five continents, where 12 000 individuals (in peacetime and leaving aside Vietnam) die of poverty each day, we can calculate that one day's freedom for Philippe Sollers* (or Régis Debray, or A.N. Other) to indulge his scribe's calling costs humanity ten children's lives ... It is not in his power, as a citizen, to stop it; but as an intellectual he can at least bear witness to it, and to illuminate his 'freedom' with the 'necessity' that kills others ... or his joy in writing with the constraints of having to feed himself which he is lucky enough to be spared – at whose expense?[119]

The final chapter dissects the 'transhistorical myth of the intellectual',[120] emphasising the negative qualities with which writers as different as Charles Maurras and Georges Sorel have associated it – disorder, insubstantiality, hypocrisy, lack of practical sense. Yet, for structural reasons argued throughout the text, the intellectual persists, and literally cannot do otherwise. Where his/her role has changed – an echo of *Le Pouvoir intellectuel* – is in its relationship with the media ('The triangle State-Media-Intelligentsia is a historically retrospective and logically operational concept ... [in which] the nature of one element cannot be modified without modifying that of the other two').[121]

This formula suggests how from this point onwards Debray's consideration of the political and of his own role as intellectual – the classic Sartrean duo – will be overdetermined by his analysis of the media. Media, for Debray, are quite literally what mediate – the word (spoken and written) and the image – and the necessary incompleteness of any social formation renders such media(tions) likewise necessary, even as their forms and manifestations change.

The notion of incompleteness is given a more extensive development in *Critique de la raison politique/A Critique of Political Reason*

* A prominent literary theorist and novelist who in the 1970s moved from a Maoist to a right-wing liberal political position, arguing from the supposed indissociability of economic and intellectual freedom.

– published in 1981, the year that Debray began by publishing in *Le Monde* (25–26 January) a eulogy of François Mitterrand entitled 'Time for respect'. That text is a curious amalgam of (what now appear) misjudgements (Mitterrand is 'faithful to his friendships and to himself'), prophetic pre-echoes ('de Gaulle today is Mitterrand'), and a reflection of Debray's longer-term preoccupations (Mitterrand is also 'the witness to a wonderful era when a leading politician could read and write'). *Critique de la raison politique* begins with a general plan so ambitious as to incite the mischievous thought that it might almost be Debray's *L'Idiot de la famille* to his Mitterrandist '*Cause du peuple*'. What emerges most clearly from the plan, as from the work, is the importance for any idea of the political of the unconscious and of what the jacket-note refers to as 'collective delirium'. One might suspect, were it not for the author's known affiliation, that this is getting into all too familiar fascist waters; but Debray's concern is with analysis not propagation, and it is of particular significance that he identifies, well *avant la lettre*, the cultural factors which were to bring about the collapse of the Eastern European régimes:

> When civil society is de facto absorbed into the Party-State, the whole of social existence is not so much controlled as frozen in the solemnity of its civic liturgies – those spectacles that constitute not the accompaniment but the essential material of everyday news (in the press, on radio or television, on posters and so forth) ... The most blinding of clichés [sc. about such societies] is that of terror, for it masks the permanent and far more dangerous characteristic of 'existing socialism', which is tedium. There have been, there are, and there will be more and more 'socialist' societies without gulags, even – a major advantage over the West – without political prisoners; the real question is whether or not we shall see the emergence of socialist societies where people are not bored.[122]

That the endless ceremonials and cults of personality in Communist régimes (Stalin, Mao, Kim Il Sung ...) were a form of secularised religion is hardly a new perception. What is disturbing about them, for Debray, is their exhausted reenactment of the most abiding kinds of political and social practice ('the problem today is not difference but permanence').[123] Francis Fukuyama may have proclaimed the 'end of history' with the supposed worldwide triumph of liberal-democratic society, but many of the old Communist régimes must have suggested that history had less ended than come to a stop, frozen in an immemorial round of mind-numbing self-exaltation.

Debray here tries to account for the failure – cultural as well as political – of Marxism. (The cultural politics of the Socialists under

Jack Lang were of a gaudy polyvalence that clearly represented a deliberate attempt to distance themselves as far as possible from Stalinist tedium, and in the process, as we shall see, succeeded in attracting Debray's opprobrium ....) One major factor that is of fundamental importance throughout his work is the centrality of the nation-state ('Marxists suffer from a problem with the nation').[124] *Critique de la raison politique* sets out to be 'a study of the conditions of organisation and functioning of stable human groups',[125] and whilst the flux of definition and redefinition of nation-states since the time at which Debray was writing has reached dizzying speed, the existence of the nation-state as a key mode of human social organisation has not (yet) been called into serious practical question. 'Marxism did perhaps inaugurate "a new kind of philosophical practice" (Althusser), but this has not given rise to a new political practice';[126] the break-up of the Soviet Union into an array of often hostile nation-states retrospectively reinforces Debray's argument. The closed philosophical system of Debray's earlier Althusserian Marxism, in this perspective, could not give rise to a new political practice, for 'political philosophy is distinguished from the philosophy of science in that it is *the science of insoluble problems*'.[127] This might seem to imply a quietistic or fatalistic detachment from any form of political involvement, but Debray makes it clear that: 'It is possible ... to consider a society without classes or state as a logically inconsistent Utopia, and at the same time the struggle for the attainment of that society as a practical imperative, although – or even because – logically "unjustifiable."'[128]

This has clear echoes of religious discourses on the constitutive irrationality of belief, from Tertullian's 'I believe because it is absurd' through to the Kierkegaardian leap of faith. It also – more soberly, more practically – points to the kind of reformist political engagement that was then Debray's, for which socialism is an informing principle or a horizon rather than a system to be scientifically constructed. Ideology, here, is to be treated with suspicion, not in the name of any weary conservative cliché about 'human nature' (a term entirely foreign to Debray's work), but because the substantive content of this or that ideology is less important for an understanding of how ideologies work than 'the mechanisms, the nature, the implications of collective adherence'.[129]

Marxism has not replaced religion, which if the latter were merely the 'opium of the people' might well have been predicted to happen:

> If religion were merely the 'inverted consciousness of the world' – a world itself inverted – we might expect it to disappear wherever the world is turned the right way up, thanks to the end of human exploitation plus free compulsory education.

> But far from fading, the old stars are everywhere shining more brightly.[130]

This observation is part of a structural analysis rather than a defeatist jeremiad; 'truth is self-sufficient, the collective by its nature is not, so that it needs a guarantor outside itself'.[131] The passionate, affective component of the political – as of adherence to any system of belief – is an integral, founding part of it ('Einstein: "everything is explicable in the world apart from the fact that the world is explicable"'[132] – reason and science themselves aporetically dependent in the last resort upon something like a leap of faith, which ensures that their systems are no more capable of operating as self-contained wholes than any others). Thus, for the philosopher Michel Serres, 'saints, geniuses, heroes, role-models, champions of all kinds do not shatter institutions, but make them possible',[133] which does not so much put forward an answer to the vexed question of why the liberating word of a Jesus Christ or a Karl Marx has given rise to such edifices of repression as suggest (pessimistically?) that it could scarcely have been otherwise. The mythical, in a literal sense the super-natural, is, in a move reminiscent of the Althussero-Lacanian stress on the inescapability of the ideological, forever imbricated with the social and the political. The evolution of Marxism from root-and-branch atheism to (at the time Debray was writing) effectively the largest of world religions is less a paradox than a structural necessity, and the identity of the nation – a reality because a myth – has been a greater agent for social change than the successive Socialist and Communist Internationals:

> each of these valiantly recited its piece, revolutionary (unificatory), rationalist (unitary) or moralistic (universalising), but the real revolutions have taken place in the wings or on a quite different scene, that of nations struggling for survival (the Paris Commune, October in Russia, the Chinese, Vietnamese and Cuban victories and so on).[134]

Debray's ominous conclusion ('The globalisation of objects = the tribalisation of subjects')[135] appears even more pertinent now, with the rise of fundamentalism – whether Muslim in the Arab world or Christian in the United States – than in 1981. It also helps to explain his abiding preoccupation with questions of weaponry and defence, which inspired three of his 1980s' works: *La Puissance et les rêves/Power and Dreams* (1984), *Les Empires contre l'Europe/Empires against Europe* (1985), and *Tous azimuts/On All Fronts* (1989). *La Puissance et les rêves* draws on his experience working for Mitterrand, who he points out had ignored the centenary of Marx's death but addressed UNESCO on that of the death of the Jesuit mystic Teilhard de Chardin in 1981 – proof if one will that socialism is a 'rational form of Messianism'.[136] It is also an eloquent plea for national self-defence:

> Justine [the – initially – innocent heroine of the Marquis de Sade's eponymous novel – trans.] must learn about power, not simply to survive in the international jungle but to impose her will without losing her soul. This is a question of life or death.[137]

His scepticism about internationalism – surprising perhaps in one of the left – is rooted in the notion of incompleteness, for 'the group made up of all finite groups is not itself a group'.[138] What this is judged to mean in practice is that international law is by definition favourable to the right, since it acts to maintain the status quo and 'by definition, a revolution is an illegal act'.[139] This, of course, all depends on how far one accepts that the performative mythical function of the nation is effectively an eternal given, and on how one defines 'revolution' (were the 'quiet revolutions' in Eastern Europe revolutionary, illegal, neither or both?). The text argues strongly for three things: a French nuclear deterrent ('the best way of preventing nuclear war is with nuclear weapons');[140] for a 'third left', neither Marxist-economist nor Christian-moralist, that will find 'the right kernel'[141] for its self-definition in the idea of the national interest; and – paradoxically – for such a rediscovered and reformulated nationalism as a means whereby the French intelligentsia might contrive to step outside its peculiarly limited vision. That vision, which privileged Poland over South Africa or Afghanistan over India, was largely determined by the fact that for most French intellectuals 'communism was the most important experience of their life',[142] and the settling of their accounts with the Soviet Union – neither a truly national nor a truly international phenomenon, whence perhaps its demise – thus determined their global political preoccupations.

That the French intelligentsia has a strong tendency towards parochialism is difficult to contest; perhaps only thus have its universalising pretensions been able to maintain themselves. Precisely how the retheorised 'national fact', or '*realpolitik* of the left',[143] Debray advocates might work to change that is insufficiently clear. He was writing at a time when, with Reaganomics and Thatcherism at the height of their ascendancy, France was in a minority among the major developed nations in having a government of the left, so that the national specificity he upholds had a very particular resonance for one closely connected with that government. It may be the conflict between short-term politics and long-term philosophy that renders *La Puissance et les rêves* in many ways an unsatisfying – dare one say incomplete? – text. This conflict is evoked in its closing pages, which deplore the increasing haste of contemporary political and diplomatic life before making the lapidary assertion that 'speed, when it is a value in itself not a means to an end, is right-wing ... Slowness is revolutionary, like memory.'[144] Margaret Thatcher and Ronald Reagan might seem to provide a self-cancelling example here, but it is clearly the meditative quality Mitterrand so sedulously cultivated as a part of his image that provides an important subtext. The 'eternal present' of politics in the media age has an inbuilt tendency to privilege image and appearance over substantive content – a leitmotif in Debray's most recent work – and thus to block or foreclose the serious reflection that is a *sine qua non* for major social change.

Les Empires contre l'Europe is a plea for something very like the Gaullian 'Europe of nation-states', with France implicitly *primus inter pares*. The 'East/West' division that governed the geopolitics of the time is described as a myth masking the domination of the USA and the Soviet Union, and the 'Soviet menace' (Mikhail Gorbachev had only just succeeded to power, and Ronald Reagan had denounced the 'evil empire' only a few years before) is demystified in a remarkably prescient passage:

> In 1985, Communism ... is a historical survival – painful in eastern Europe, more and more uncomfortable elsewhere, in countries where 'socialism' has not simply fallen in behind the Soviet army (China, Cuba, Yugoslavia, Vietnam, etc.). Bereft of its motive force, Communism is no longer 'the major question for humanity today' (Edgar Morin): as members of a divided Europe, it is of concern to us, but as far-sighted intellectuals, there is no need for it to obsess us. The most aggressive totalitarian expansion of today – the only one with the demography to match its ambitions – wears the colours of Islam and makes its canon law the source of all civil law.[145]

With American influence expanding and that of the Soviet Union contracting, Debray fears 'the Finlandisation of Europe'[146] – its effective reduction to a satellite of the USA – yet does not adopt the kind of 'pan-European' approach to which this might have been expected to lead. National specificity is imperilled by the Americanisation of culture – the specificity of a universalising, state-centred, republican France grounded in a culture of writing:

> [sc. We must] think together the state which is losing the competence to be competent and the intelligentsia which is losing the means to be intelligent; the degradation of the idea of the universal in the instruction and production of French minds, and of the *difference* of France in the concert of nations; the weakening of French specificity in the Atlantic order with that of the state in our civil society, of the republican idea in national life, of schooling in the collective imagination, of history and

philosophy in education ('those who do not remember the past are condemned to repeat it').[147]

This 'certain idea of France' (de Gaulle) is precisely what Debray was to see eroded in the latter part of Mitterrand's presidency, against which *Que vive la République!* and *A demain de Gaulle!* are, we shall see, covert polemics. The Soviet Union no longer represents a real danger, for it 'does not have enough software or imagery to offer';[148] but imaginary dangers are in their way 'real' enough, serving as they do to bind social groups together in a fear that is the product of their necessary incompleteness ('a society is not only a "collective dream": it is first and foremost a collective fear ... each "we" comes about through the "them" it confronts').[149] This means, for Debray, that a nation can only be said to exist in so far as it has the means – literal and military as well as cultural and symbolic – of defending itself. There has never been a peace movement in France comparable to the Campaign for Nuclear Disarmament in Britain, largely because the French deterrent, since the withdrawal from NATO in 1966, has always been perceived as guarantor of national independence rather than a threat to it. Debray's hawkishness is thus less anomalous than it might appear, undershoring as it does his perception of France as 'the only medium-sized country to have the capacities of a world power'[150] – thanks to its military strength as much as (and, importantly, at the same time as) its technological, linguistic and cultural prominence. His vision of a neo-Gaullian (preferably) socialist-led Europe of nation-states would of course be dramatically altered today by German unification even more than by the final collapse of the Soviet Union; *secundus inter pares* somchow lacks the requisite mythic resonance ... The text concludes with a renunciation of political writing (presumably coincident with his resignation as adviser to Mitterrand), and a weary Romantic palinode that reads like a parody of itself:

> I regard politics, that universe made up of things that each day seem to us less significant than they did the day before, as the booby-trap of human ambition; 'current affairs' for me means what does not last, and I am attracted only to what does – songs, films, Requiem Masses, paintings, love.[151]

This in turn leads to a questioning of his long-standing attachment to political writing, born *inter alia* of an increasing disillusionment with the persuasive power of anything he might publish ('The more complex and elaborate a work is, the less easily presentable, readable and communicable it will be (three hours of work = 300 000 consumers, three months = 30 000, thirty years = 300)'[152] – an argument evocative of *Le Pouvoir intellectuel en France*). That attachment is traced back in the last resort, not to ethical or ideological origins (the archetypal Sartrean duo), but to the 'national fact', in a passage remarkable for its transition from an almost Maurrasian-sounding assertion of transcendental identity to a defence of the indissociability of the importance of the state and the liberties it guarantees:

> My real reason stems from a clan morality – from an obscure sense of belonging, which means that my conscious self is not everything ... and that my time is not all my own, that some of it belongs to my country, because I owe it a debt that I am happy to be obliged to pay. It also has to do with the conviction that I live in a precarious, precious and rare society, whose rarity is guaranteed by a state with an uncertain future, and that that state is France's most precious possession, because it guarantees our freedoms – notably that to be ourselves – with our collective difference, our singular, multi-timbred voice in the 'concert of nations'. It would be fatal to dissociate the question of individual and public freedoms from that of [sc. national] identity.[153]

The centrality of the state – a major target, be it remembered, of Thatcherism and Reaganomics – has since the Revolution been more pronounced in France than in any other major nation, and for that very reason has come under regular if generally ineffectual attack from the French right (Édouard Balladur, former prime minister and an economic disciple of Thatcherism, published in 1987 a book entitled *Je crois en l'homme plus qu'en l'état/I believe in Man rather than in the State*). The import of Debray's text is thus less reactionary than it might appear, though his failure to define what a 'nation' is other than performatively, as a myth commanding *de facto* acceptance, is disturbing. It is, however, partly accounted for in his own terms of reference, for which the most conspicuous theoretical and practical failure of Marxism has been its incapacity to overcome or engage effectively with nationalism ('there will be never be a Communist supranationality').[154]

This failure forms part of the background to *Tous azimuts*, which is dealt with here out of direct chronological sequence because it forms the sequel to the two previously-discussed works (and its author's most flagrant breach, to date, of his vow of political silence). Written in response to a commission from the French National Defence Foundation to 'reflect upon the great lines of force which, with the new course of events in the East, might form those of European defence',[155] *Tous azimuts* distils what will by now be familiar preoccupations of its author: the importance of culture and defence in defining a collectivity ('there are two ways to X-ray the soul of Europe – by questioning it about its culture and its defence'),[156] that, closely connected, of an independent French deterrent as a block to potential Germano-Soviet hegemony within Europe, and the return of the crucial importance of the nation:

> The German Federal Republic was not born in 1949 as a nation, but to forget the idea of nationhood in the affirmation of a European democratic ideal. That time is drawing to a close, especially in Germany. The Europe of nations and of minorities, buried in the history books like a bad dream, is with us once more.[157]

Five years on, it seems possible to say that the 'European democratic ideal' (the European Union and Maastricht) and the 'Europe of nations and minorities' (united Germany, partitioned Czechoslovakia ...) share an uneasy coexistence. Within that shifting field of forces, Debray sees the France of 1989 as particularly well placed to take a leading initiative in 'a just and durable order of peace for the whole of Europe',[158] thanks to its possession of an independent nuclear deterrent and a democratic-socialist government with 'a vision of the future at least as honourable as that of the Soviet leader, and more solidly grounded'.[159]

European defence, for Debray, must be multi- not trans-national ('Europe does not make Europeans dream, and all the rest flows from that').[160] The notion of a '*tous azimuts*' defence – one that faces in all directions, prepared to deter or protect against conflicts and attacks from whatever quarter – stands in contrast to the bipolar (which is to say Eastward-facing) system characteristic of the Cold War years. The echoes of de Gaulle in all this are not difficult to detect – who else in modern French history has so powerfully combined a passion for the theory and practice of defence with an internationalist idea, however contestable, of the nation? – but it is a de Gaulle (as Debray's will always be) a very long way from what passes for 'Gaullism' in the France of today. The mixture of nationalistic rhetoric and a fascination with military history that characterises Debray's work on defence makes it probably the hardest part of his work to empathise with, but it is an extremely important part of that work nevertheless.

Nationhood and weaponry, we have seen, were fundamental to Debray's experience in Latin America; the form in which these preoccupations recur in his mid and late 1980s' writing may give pause for surprise, but that recurrence suggests how much of a piece his *oeuvre* is, through its variety of guises and genres.

CHAPTER 3

Autobiography, Republicanism and Gaullism: The Work of the Late 1980s

Debray's passion for literary and artistic culture found expression in the publication of *Éloges/Eulogies* in 1986. This collection of essays ranges from Tintoretto (already the subject of a study by Sartre, with whose view of him as a painter of human existential abandonment Debray takes issue) through writers all more or less influential on Debray's work. These include the dissident Marxist novelist Victor Serge, André Malraux, whose comic exaggeration of his exploits in the Spanish Civil War does not preclude him from having 'the best eye in contemporary literature'[161] along with Claude Simon, and Gabriel García Márquez whose masterpiece *One Hundred Years of Solitude* is the best-known Latin American novel in the West.

The major shift in Debray's work at this time, however, is to be found in his two autobiographical texts, *Comète, ma comète/Comet, my Comet* and *Les Masques/Masks*. The former (1986) is a wryly affectionate account of his relations with his daughter (Céline), compared by Michel Contat in *Le Monde* (4 July 1986) when it appeared to texts as different as *Kramer versus Kramer*, Serge Gainsbourg's cinematic exploration of his near-incestuous passion for his daughter (*La Passion Charlotte*), and Jacques Doillon's film *La Vie de famille*, in which a divorced father (Sami Frey) takes his daughter on an impromptu holiday in Spain and explores their relationship with the aid of a videocamera. It is also the text in which Debray identifies, in a manner reminiscent of Sartre, the moment at which his future destiny was determined – in Ecuador in 1964, when embarrassment and shame overcame his disgust at a couple of US tourists throwing money at poor peasants and photographing their scrambling for it as if it were a huge joke:

> If I had strangled that stupid bitch on the spot and grabbed the camera from that arsehole, if I had dared to shout, stamp my feet and box on the spot instead of flapping my fins like a fish out of water – I should not have needed to stay in the area to purge that affront and expiate that blasphemy ... If I had had more presence of mind, I should have been able to take up my natural course and go from the rue d'Ulm to Harvard or

> Princeton as a visiting professor, like everybody else ... and, back in time for May 1968, I would have put some Maoism in my tank, Raymond Aron would have picked me out shortly afterwards and I would have been photographed with Jean-Paul Sartre.[162]

It would probably not be wrong to detect a note of 'there but for the grace of God ...' in Debray's ironic evocation of the moment that sealed, in a manner that can properly be described as religious, his affinity with the Latin American poor by impelling him to atone for the insult visited upon them. This is presented in the form of a monologue to his daughter/confidante, sometimes also addressed as 'comrade' ('my child is the only creature I can cherish without worshipping'),[163] and his promise, after a visit to the Palais de la Découverte (Parisian equivalent to the London planetarium), to take her to watch the next appearance of Halley's Comet in 2062 ('The first one there can queue up for the other')[164] bespeaks a transcendental confidence unlike anything in his work hitherto. Michel Contat observed in *Le Monde* of 4 July 1986: '"All children are the mirrors of death", said Sartre, who took good care not to have any.' Debray counterposes to this the suggestion that they may equally well be the mirrors of immortality, the more so for being the only ones we have.

Les Masques appeared in the following year (1987), as Debray was preparing to leave Mitterrand's service for a post at the Conseil d'État – the body that pronounces on whether projected new laws are compatible with the French constitution, and hears complaints from citizens against public officials. His (albeit reluctantly) proclaimed political affiliation since has been as a 'republican', understood not as a supporter of Ronald Reagan or George Bush but in a strictly French sense as an upholder of the lay institutions and written constitution of the French Republic.[165] The move (which took place in 1988) from an obviously partisan political appointment to one much more explicitly associated with the republican tradition is clearly of a piece with this shift in – or reformulation of – Debray's political self-definition.

Little or none of this, however, appears in *Les Masques* – for me along with *Le Pouvoir intellectuel en France* the most remarkable of Debray's texts, and one that places itself in a French autobiographical tradition that might be said to take as its object the private self – or selves – of the public writer. Rousseau's *Confessions* is the obvious archetype of this tradition (though the textual weaving-together of private and public, of the autobiographical and the conceptual, goes back even further, to Montaigne and Pascal), whose most influential twentieth-century examples are almost certainly Beauvoir's *Mémoires* and Sartre's *Les Mots*. Debray's title bears the intertextual imprint of Sartre's, much as does Althusser's bizarre and delirious 'autobiographical' memoir *Les Faits*, written in 1976 but not published until after his death in 1992 along with *L'Avenir dure longtemps*. The latter text, recounting Althusser's murder of his wife in 1980 and the tormented life that had led up to it, has certainly been the most notorious in recent times of the autobiographical genre under discussion. Barthes's *Incidents* and *Soirées de Paris* – jottings about his homosexual experiences in Morocco and Paris respectively – and Derrida's *Circonfession* (published as part of his and Geoffrey Bennington's *Jacques Derrida*), which speaks of his early life and in particular of the trauma of his circumcision, can be seen as other significant contributions to it.

It is no coincidence that such autobiographical writing has latterly come so powerfully to the fore. Critical theory, especially in the 'Marxist-Freudian' form so characteristic of it in France from Lévi-Strauss onwards, was often (and erroneously) taken to deny the individual or even render him/her superfluous. What it, and its successors, in fact did was to call the idea of an invariant human nature into complex and ceaseless question. Individuals were constituted by the social groupings – microcosmic (this or that family) and macrocosmic (this or that society) – into which they were born and in which they lived, and the relations of kinship (Lévi-Strauss, Lacan), class (Althusser), power (Foucault), gender (Hélène Cixous, Luce Irigaray), and language (all the above and arguably more than any of them Derrida) determined their subjectivity and their sense of (one, more or no) identity/ies. That is an oversimplification, but here it will have to do.[166]

In *Les Masques*, Debray interrogates his own subjectivity through the unfolding of a – the? – classic late twentieth-century intellectual identity crisis, classic because at once political and emotional. (I say 'late twentieth-century', but the examples of Sartre, Malraux, even Rousseau are there to suggest that the phenomenon goes back beyond World War Two as far as the Enlightenment.) The text begins with the revelation that 'Silvia Murillo' (in real life Carmen Castillo, the widow of the Colombian revolutionary militant Camilo Torres), Debray's lover for several years in the early and mid 1970s, had had another partner for many of these years, the father of the son Debray had believed to be his. 'The only creature in the world in whom I trusted entirely ... had for years been deceiving me' – a trauma that went beyond the 'mere' pain of love lost to shatter the foundations of Debray's sense of self ('The revelation that one is no longer loved torments, lacerates, burns, but does not mutilate. The revelation that what one has believed to be true was false is something quite different.')[167] This unfolding tale of 'sadism of the intelligence, masochism of the libido'[168] – a term applied to Althusser, but with an evident reference to Debray himself, and one which reads oddly like an affective reinscription of Gramsci's 'pessimism of the intelligence, optimism of the will' – is set in the context of a life that spans the Latin America of the 1960s (the relationship of Castro and Guevara is seen as 'the most beautiful story of friendship I have been lucky enough to encounter in my short life')[169] and the France of the 1970s and 1980s (Althusser makes an appearance gardening 'like an old child of the jungle'[170] in Debray's country house in the Ile-de-France).

The risk such an undertaking inevitably entails is that of reducing the public stage of politics and culture (Simone Signoret and Joan Baez play important roles here alongside more obviously 'political' figures) to a mere backdrop for the 'real', because personal, (hi)story of an affectivity – a risk even more marked now than when the work appeared because of the falling-off of militant political activity. Debray makes it plain that on the contrary 'I do not want in revealing my own little (hi)story to deny history on the larger scale – it is the threads that weave them together that I want to bring to light.'[171] Given the very public nature of his 'own little (hi)story', and the roots of his relationship with 'Silvia' in the Latin American struggles, this is a less daunting undertaking than it might appear, and any suggestion of the gossip-column or of name-dropping in these pages where García Márquez, Poulantzas, Bernard Kouchner, Gaston Defferre appear cheek by jowl seems to me as it were redeemed in advance by the hideous cry of suffering and loss of belief on which the work opens. ('My foundations were spurious, my inner kernel of cardboard, my past a long deception ... I neither applauded nor accused; I simply sank.')[172]

In so despairing a situation, in a Paris in which psychoanalysis was all but *de rigueur*, the couch might have been expected to beckon; but the classical – dare I say 'Cartesian'? – cast of thought which (perhaps never more than here) often provides an austere counterpoint to Debray's verbal effulgence was clearly resolutely hostile to such an idea:

> I have little trust in shamans who take fifty pounds from some poor devil to get him to talk about Mummy and Daddy for ten minutes on a couch ... I trusted what is known as truth – the inheritance of my good philosophical education and of the lies socially in force.[173]

Debray declares himself to have remained untouched by the enthusiasm for Lacanian and post-Lacanian psychoanalysis for so long prevalent in France – something the pungent populism he affects in the above passage might in any event have led one to suspect. Yet *Les Masques*, like the autobiographical tradition of which it forms part, is necessarily something of a 'talking [or at any rate a writing] cure', deploying language all at once to heal, to exorcise, to dissimulate and to reveal. That would not be a bad account either of the manner in which François Mitterrand has over the years used his undoubted linguistic mastery (could Debray's aversion to psychoanalysis have something to do with his lengthy involvement with practical politics, as though one sort of institutionalised linguistic bad faith were as much as one individual could take?), and it is interesting that the pages of *Les Masques* devoted to Mitterrand speak as much of the private man as of the public figure. The President's 'left-wing temperament and right-wing culture' are presented as the mirror-image of Debray's own, and his pragmatism – that of a 'socialist who distrusts societal projects' – all but makes of him a realist novelist *manqué*:

> He sets more store by live detail than by general explanation, by perception than by theory, by people than by myths; his wisdom has over the years shed the baggage of knowledge. His best friends are writers, not teachers.[174]

The tormented Left Bank intellectual's nostalgic envy for the literary culture and rootedness of 'a man who stands upright on the earth [and] ... knows nothing of depression or indigestion'[175] is almost physically perceptible. Debray's enthusiasm for Mitterrand had a twofold basis: on the one hand, in *realpolitik* (cf. the *Lettre ouverte*), on the other, in a shared passion for words and for literary culture. Both these were to be sorely tried, by Mitterrand's failure to engage in fundamental structural reform of French society ('He opened the windows wide and let in much-needed fresh air, but he did not move any of the furniture' – Debray in personal conversation), and by the mediatic vulgarisation of his second term. Debray is particularly scathing, in an article co-authored with the painter Gérard Fromanger, about the Jean-Paul Goude inspired extravaganza to celebrate the bicentenary of the 1789 Revolution:

> Goude freed himself of the 'pretext' of 1789 as history teaching has done from chronology, geography from maps, painting from draughtmanship, mathematics from arithmetic and literature from the study of texts – and *as socialism in power has done from the pretext of socialism* [my italics]. The theatre director figures higher on the poster than the author of the play, manner swallows up matter, and illustrators come before discoverers. The kingdom of design in all its aspects is bursting with beautiful bodywork without engines. We deserved this parade.[176]

This passage merits quoting at some length because it focuses attention on the major contradiction by which Debray's most recent work is informed – that between nostalgia for a time when culture was primarily verbal and politics rooted in ideas and discussion, and a historically-grounded realisation that such a time is past, never (at least as itself) to return. This break has most commonly been articulated by writers and theoreticians of post-modernism (Jean-François Lyotard's *La Condition post-moderne/The Post-Modern Condition* and Fredric Jameson's *The Political Unconscious* remain the key texts here), but Debray's work distinguishes itself markedly from the postmodern 'genre' through its refusal to celebrate the new era of the visual and the image. The particular form of institutionalised bad faith – that defining attribute of the intellectual – that permeates the later Debray takes the form of nostalgia – not for an age of ideological certainties (whatever else, Debray is not a sheepishly repentant Stalinist) but for one of ideas articulated in and through words.

He has claimed (in conversation) to be less of an intellectual than he may appear, because of his abiding fascination with weapons and with images. The first is of a piece with his preoccupation with the nation-state and his experience (not shared by most leftist intellectuals) of real armed struggle, the second is clearly Janus-faced, beguiled by the visual image at the same time as deploring, with an evident sense of historically-determined powerlessness, its hegemony.

The affectionate references to Balzac at the beginning of *Le Pouvoir intellectuel en France* ('No entry here if you are not a Balzacian')[177] become perhaps more existentially comprehensible in this light; Balzac's simultaneous fascination and disgust with the expansive rapacity of early mercantile capitalism found expression through a cleaving to the *ancien régime* that was clearly historically doomed ('Engels showed that Balzac, although his political creed was legitimist royalism, nevertheless inexorably exposed the vices and weakness of royalist feudal France and described its death agony with magnificent poetic vigour').[178] In like manner, perhaps, Debray's intellectual creed may be verbal and conceptual, yet the texts he produces to proclaim, defend or historically situate it also inevitably tend to suggest that it is forever deprived of the hegemony it once exercised – a hegemony whose ascendancy and fall are both figured in the career of François Mitterrand.

For Debray, that hegemony still appears defendable (as well as defensible) in the republican tradition with which he identifies himself. The key texts here are *Que vive la République!/Long Live the Republic!* and the article (originally published in the left-wing weekly *Le Nouvel Observateur*) *République ou Démocratie/Republic or Democracy*. Both, significantly, date from 1989 and the bicentennial – described by Debray as 'that sumptuous repression'[179] for its meretricious deployment of the images and icons of revolution in such a way as to drain them of all substantive content. The article contrasts the Republic – upheld by reason, grounded in institutions and law, governed by universal considerations – with a 'democracy' upheld by production and property, grounded in nothing more substantial than communication and contract, and increasingly at the mercy of local or partial interests (Margaret Thatcher's Britain, then still in its atomisatory pomp, would serve excellently as an example of this). It is the republican privileging of the universal over the particular that leads Debray in this piece to take an extremely hard line over the 'headscarf affair', in which three Muslim girls were excluded from class because they insisted on wearing their headscarves, in violation of the secular principle whereby overt signs of religious affiliation are deemed to have no place in the state educational system:

> What if, for example, a young Muslim girl is refused admission to a classroom unless she leaves her veil in the cloakroom? 'The right thing to do', cries the Republican. 'No, quite the wrong one!' says the democrat indignantly. 'Secularity', one will say. 'Intolerance', the other will reply ... A squabble over words? No: a fundamental misunderstanding of principles.[180]

Debray's adherence to the republican principle receives more extensive development in *Que vive la République!*, which early in the second Mitterrand term struck a more jarring note than may at first appear. That period of French political life was dominated by a 'cohabitation' between Mitterrand and his prime minister and bitter Socialist Party rival Michel Rocard scarcely less hostile than the one between Mitterrand and Jacques Chirac that had preceded it. The 'Mitterrand/Rocard years' were marked by a process of 'opening' to include ministers from opposition parties or without party affiliation and by the concomitant promotion of the Rocardian ideal of 'civil society' – in Debray's terms emphatically a 'democratic' ideal rather than a republican one, and one fraught with perils for the republican values of law and the nation-state. The republican state is for Debray necessarily a national one, concretised first and foremost at its foundation by 'the unprecedented creation of a popular Army as an instrument of upward social mobility and national cohesion'[181] – a view by now familiar from his texts on defence. The task of the contemporary nation-state is crisply defined – 'to lay claim to the role of counter-power to civil society, much as Education might do to Television, Politics to Economy, Law to Money'.[182] It is in this context that his diatribe against consensus should be understood – a diatribe that can also be read as a disabused parting of the ways with a 'socialist' régime which by then was all too clearly, through 'opening' and in many other ways, in pursuit of nothing more challenging than the lowest common denominator:

> A consensual society is a dead society. Consensus preserves, that is what it is for. It naturally favours the side of order and thus of the strong ... We are on the side of the weak – on the 'wrong' side. We are there precisely to break with consensus and turn losers into winners, to propose reforms which by definition the majority does not want, for if it did they would already have taken place, to disturb slumbers, rock the boat, sow turbulence and dissonance where everything seems just as usual. People in our movement are surely called upon to broaden *areas of dissent*. That is what they are there for. There are always enough people to prance around the garden of consensus. If our ancestors had become smitten with this orthodoxy ... you would not be there today to preside over the Bastille celebrations.[183]

The 'you' apostrophised in that final sentence is of course Mitterrand, whose drift towards consensus politics is closely connected with the increasing domination of the visual media over the culture of politics, the state and the printed word of which he comes to seem the last major French representative. The 'régime of direct mediocracy' that lies just around the corner will have as its corollary 'an ex-people, rechristened the audience or the public ... which will thereby have lost its unity and even its reality'.[184] The 'people' in question is that which under the successive French Republics has been legally and constitutionally sovereign; the 'audience' or 'public' – an atomised array of individuals sitting in front of their television or computer screen – marks in a sense that goes far beyond the economic the galloping privatisation of society, at once effect and cause of the now dominant 'videosphere'. Debray's choice lights upon 13 May 1968 as the starting date of 'postmodern democracy', 'separating archaic past from mediatic future'[185] – a curmudgeonly response to the events of that month, to be sure, but one also which recognises that the immense cultural shift they heralded and embodied was not so unmixed a blessing as it may have appeared.

Humanitarianism and terrorism, for Debray, are the twin legacy of the consensual 'media-system', flattening out the complexities of society and history into a simple bipolar reaction that can engender an illusion of togetherness among individuals sitting each in front of their own television screen. 'The discourse of realities is a complex one, but the simplest are the ones that go down best';[186] far easier to anathematise the IRA and send a cheque to Oxfam like everyone else, after all, than to engage seriously (as a genuine political culture would) with the reasons why those two organisations – and others – exist.

Debray's political loyalties in *Que vive la République!* remain clearly defined, in what an English-speaking public might well recognise as Orwellian terms:

> For a century, those who are inspired by justice, and more precisely by the egalitarian ideal, have been divided into three groups. The far or ultra-left: it has a system of thought, but it has never held power, so that system cannot be verified. The Communist left has had a system of thought and held power; we know what that has meant. The socialist or social-democratic left is the only one to have wielded state power without piling up massacres and economic disasters.[187]

Such a left, however, cannot for Debray long survive in any recognisable or coherent form the erosion of state power by civil society and the mediocracy. His republicanism appears not merely as of the left, but as (within his own problematic) virtually the only kind of left it remains meaningful to defend.

It is in this light that *A demain de Gaulle!/De Gaulle for Tomorrow!* of 1990 – English translation *Charles de Gaulle: Futurist of the Nation* – needs to be read. This more than any other text has earned Debray the reputation of being a political turncoat, slithering opportunistically from Third World *gauchisme* in the 1960s, by way of social democracy and what the French call 'Mitterrandolatry', to a final throwing in of his lot with the nationalistic right. Such a reading is a travesty, for as we have already seen Debray had precious little in common with 1960s' *gauchisme* (he has spoken in conversation of his 'mental exclusion of the use of violence in Western Europe'), and the use he makes of de Gaulle in his recent work is a polemical, mythical one (he has spoken too of an 'idealised de Gaulle') that has nothing whatever to do with the politicians that call themselves 'Gaullist' in France today. This mythical de Gaulle – mythical as Napoleon, Lenin, even in his own way Mitterrand, have at different times been for their partisans – is characterised above all by his cleaving to a verbal and literary culture and his vision of a 'Europe of nations' – which is to say emphatically not a federal one. 'The universe of words was his great preoccupation',[188] and this was closely linked with his political activity and its abiding sense of History (the capital H is intentional), for:

> He says that the state becomes real only through memories and memoirs, the living being of a nation becomes flesh through the text. An action is not legitimate because public opinion approves it at the time; it acquires value through its sense, or in other words its inscription in the panoramic unfolding of a very long adventure.[189]

We are on what will by now be familiar territory here – the indissociability of history, writing and the state, implicitly contrasted with the 'eternal present' of the image and civil society. Debray's text, written in response to a commission (the Institut Charles de Gaulle asked him and other intellectuals of the left to produce texts on their response to the General), acquires considerable polemical force through its contrast between de Gaulle and the Mitterrand of the second term. It is as though de Gaulle served as a prism for Debray to concentrate his denunciation of Mitterrand's complicity with the mediocracy:

> What François Mitterrand called in 1971 *Le Socialisme du possible/The Socialism of the Possible* has become, twenty years later, economic liberalism tempered with the rhetoric of hope. The great coalition of those who, after 1968, said 'No' to the way things were has degraded twenty years later into a verbose, shameful 'Yes' to the way things have to be. What would people have thought of a Radical president under the Third Republic who had allowed the Church to win back secular education? Much the same as of a Socialist president under the Fifth Republic who after two terms allowed advertising to swallow up television, our form of universal education.
>
> To resurrect in this context the man whose appeal of 18 June 1940 inspired the Resistance is to bring the left-winger within us back to the surface, back to the intellectual and moral sources of that 'No', to the secret key to our reasons for existing.[190]

I have quoted this passage at unusual length because it seems to me to distil much of what is both most fascinating and most objectionable about *A demain de Gaulle!*: the denunciation of the compromises and bad faith that increasingly marked post-1981 Socialist governments, the unwavering condemnation of mediatic shallowness and venality, the obscurantist – and thus potentially highly dangerous – rhetoric of appeals to the 'secret key to reasons for existing', the convenient vagueness about whether acquiescence in media hegemony was a bowing to the historically inevitable or an irredeemable betrayal of the republican-socialist heritage. De Gaulle's own use of television was of shameless Bonapartist straightforwardness, as the simplest and most nakedly functional form of what Althusser called 'Ideological State Apparatus'; if French television has always lagged spectacularly behind the standards of public service broadcasting in Britain, he cannot escape much of the responsibility. The contrast between de Gaulle's attitude towards television and that of his British contemporary for nearly five years, prime minister Harold Wilson, is revelatory. Television may be for Debray 'our form of universal education', but it was surely not for reasons of technological underdevelopment alone that nothing like Britain's Open University was ever set up in France. 'The last West European statesman to have taken intellectual strength seriously'[191] clearly saw how the televisual image could reinforce – or, unchecked, menace – political power, but there is little evidence that he understood how it could contribute to that very intellectual strength by which he set such store.

As head of the provisional government at the Liberation, de Gaulle had refused to pardon the fascist writer and intellectual Robert Brasillach, editor of the leading collaborationist journal *Je suis partout*, who was shot in 1945. Debray asserts that this refusal, 'because writing is an act and any conscious man is accountable for his acts, was a sign of high esteem for the printed word'[192] – an argument with distinctly Sartrean echoes. On de Gaulle's later refusal to pardon Bastien-Thierry, the Army colonel responsible for the plot to assassinate him as a reprisal for the 'betrayal' of French Algeria, Debray is silent; adherence to the 'officer and gentleman' code of honour evidently fitted his argument less well than 'high esteem for the printed word'.

Debray ascribes his belated turning to de Gaulle (who had intervened on his behalf with the Bolivian government) to a rereading of the syntax of history. Concepts such as 'revolution' or 'democracy' are no longer for him, as they have overwhelmingly been for the French intelligentsia, the subjects of history. That distinction now belongs, as de Gaulle had seen all along, to the nation ('Something preexisted the quality of democracy, as before that the quality of revolution, and will survive them – something older, more active, more lasting, known for some time by the vague name of "nation"').[193]

Such an assertion needs to be understood within that French context for which nation and state have always been so indissolubly welded – though even then, as the example of right-wing French nationalist thinker Charles Maurras is there to show, it is not exempt from dangerous obscurantism.

The concept of the nation has long been a thorny one for the European left, owing largely to the inheritance of Stalinism in the immediately postwar period and the complexity of 'national liberation struggles' (from Ireland to the former Yugoslavia) since. A good deal of left-wing thinking, from Trotskyist internationalism to the pious hope for a united states of Europe, may be suspected of drawing much of its impetus from the wish that that tiresome yet seemingly irrepressible entity, the nation-state, would have the good grace to allow itself for once at least to be transcended. That hope probably seemed better founded at the time Debray wrote *A demain de Gaulle!* than now. However unsatisfactory, dangerous even, Debray's more provocatively mythopoeic formulations are, there is a chilling accuracy to his prognosis when he speaks of 'Russia, a continental country which intends to become so once more, Germany in the heart of Europe, intending to reconstruct Central Europe, and America, the world's greatest island, which is what it intends to remain'.[194] Two of those three names were still 'only' geographical realities when Debray wrote thus; their reemergence as nation-states emphasises that the disappearance of the nation is still (at best) a very long way off.

CHAPTER 4

Towards Mediology: The Work of the 1990s

Since 1992, when he left the Conseil d'État, Debray has been a full-time professional writer, though he organised the French pavilion at the Seville Universal Exhibition of that year to celebrate the 500th anniversary of the discovery of the Americas. *Christophe Colomb, le visiteur de l'aube/Christopher Columbus, the Daybreak Visitor*, published the year before, muses on Columbus's *folie de grandeur* and on the perennial marginality of Latin America ('not a participant in the world game of power – only in that of rhetoric and, sometimes, emotion').[195]

Of much greater significance, however, is *Cours de médiologie générale/A Course in General Mediology*, of 1991. In this text, Debray finally brings to fruition the project he had been nurturing ever since *Le Pouvoir intellectuel en France* – that of producing an analytical and critical taxonomy of communicative media. The jacket-note gives a good working definition of Debray's project:

> *Mediology* is the study of the material mediations through which a Word becomes flesh, an idea a collective force, a message a vision of the world ... This may illuminate the crucial, and 'words' or 'the role of ideas in history', by reconciling culture with its own materiality.

This project evokes a variety of others – not only McLuhanist or postmodern discourses on communication, but rather more interestingly the performative linguistics of J.L. Austin (whose *How to do Things with Words* has been very influential in France); Foucault, for whom power is the necessary condition and common denominator of all forms of symbolic efficacy, Michel Serres, whose *Hermès ou la communication/Hermes or Communication* interrogates the modes and conditions under which communication becomes possible, and even Marx's approach (never codified in a single major text) to questions of art, literature and their relationship with power. Marx posing himself the question of how Greek epic poetry can still be read in capitalist society ('... is the *Iliad* possible at all when the printing press and even printing machines exist?'),[196] and answering that the very naivety of humanity's historical childhood ensures our abiding pleasure in its works, has more than a little in common with the Debray who writes that 'there is in our souls, simultaneously, a calligraphic East, a printed Europe, and a big-screen America, and these continents continually negotiate within us their respective places'.[197]

Marx, on the other hand, proclaimed as a scientific truth the primacy of the economic in human social affairs, whereas in Debray's later work it is increasingly the cultural – even the religious – that predominates. This is assimilated, in one of his very rare references to psychoanalysis, to the Freudian unconscious:

> ... the mental economy of any grouping can be compared to a system of three levels, each of a different kind and fulfilling a different function. There is an archaic religious infrastructure, the basis of any collective sensibility, which evolves very slowly over a long time-span; a variable ideological stratum, rationally expressible in the mid-term, a set of hypotheses that structure a vision of the world; and finally a strategic layer, a narrow strip turned towards the future, represented by ideal constructions, societal projects, and explicit, coherent, attacking theses in the short term. It is easy to recognise the little [sic] Freudian machinery; the religious corresponds to the unconscious, the ideological to the preconscious, and the political to the conscious. When these three levels come into conflict, it is the first – the unconscious – that will triumph in the last resort.[198]

This variation on the theme of incompleteness suggests that the material symbols by which humans live, and thus the media in which these symbols are articulated and disseminated, ultimately determine their social existence. If 'politics is no longer in command', this has less to do with any Fukuyamaesque or postmodernist espousal of the 'end of history' (or even of ideology), than with the fact that 'the sphere of *circulation* of ideas and representations directly commands their *production*'.[199] Victor Hugo's Claude Frollo in *Notre-Dame de Paris*, holding a book whilst contemplating his beloved cathedral and realising that '*this will kill that. The book will kill the building*'[200] – that mass literacy and the printing press would render the medieval 'bibles in stone' superfluous – can claim to be one of the first mediologists. He is indeed explicitly evoked by Debray, who then updates him by way of a novelist's fantasy about a Communist 'archdeacon' in May 1968 ('The branch secretary contemplated the monumental glass building in silence, then, stretching one hand out with a sigh towards the television set on the table and the other towards the Communist Party headquarters, said: "Alas, this will kill that."'). The 'privatisation' of culture brought about by new audiovisual technologies is the reason why 'the audiovisual tends to the "right" as the printed word does to the "left"'.[201]

This is a stimulating, even a tempting, hypothesis, but one against which there are at least two important things to be said. In the first place, technologies determine ideas, to be sure, but in a complex, dialectical, far from innocent manner; the privatisation of culture in Britain during the Thatcher years, for example, went ahead as rapidly as it did because it fitted a political and ideological agenda explicitly hostile to the very concepts of a public sphere and public space. Secondly, and complementarily, it is by no means certain that the 'videosphere' will continue to evolve in the same ideological direction as that in which it has hitherto been propelled. Debray says as much when he points out that authoritarian regimes in the Third World today fear the spread of video exactly as their medieval European counterparts did that of printing:

> It subverts official propaganda, gets round religious bans (particularly Muslim ones) and is becoming a political weapon for the various forms of opposition ... Video is even more dangerous for the authorities in developing countries than the book once was for us.[202]

In the West, meanwhile, the advent of the CD-ROM, and soon doubtless the interactive multi-media CD, may well literally reinscribe the 'printed' word, enabling a coexistence of logo/grapho/videosphere that could even refute Debray's assertion that '"socialism", viable in a typographic milieu ... cannot reproduce itself outside: the audiovisual niche is fatal to it'.[203] Even to put forward, however tentatively, such a possibility as I have done is to give a considerable hostage to fortune, but no more so than Debray's mediological theses themselves.

These theses are expressed in diagrammatic form at the end of *Cours de médiologie générale* – a diagram I reproduce in full since it provides the most lucid and comprehensive outline of Debray's mediological thought from (about) the time of *Le Pouvoir intellectuel en France* onwards.

What Debray has here given us – and he is among the first thinkers, if not actually the first, to do so – is a taxonomy of social formations (1789 and 1968 serving as the cut-off points between them) overdetermined, as the Althusserian in him might (have) put it, by their dominant medium of communication. The supposed erstwhile priority of creation over mediation (which diminishes as we move from left to right on the above table) may now appear less to be mourned, as it was in that reluctant swansong to the graphosphere *Le Pouvoir intellectuel en France*, than to have been – as for Derrida the traditional Western priority of speech over writing – an illusion all along. Creation, like the social formations

	Writing (Logosphere)
Strategic Milieu (Protection of Power)	The Earth
Group Ideal (and Political Tendency)	The One (City, Kingdom, Empire) – absolutism
Form and Vector of Time	Circle (the eternal, repetition) – archeocentric
Canonical Age	Old Age
Paradigm of Attraction	Mythos (mysteries, dogmas, epics)
Dominant Symbolic Mode	Religions (theology)
Spiritual Class Holding Sacred Power in Society	Church (prophets and clerics Dogma is sacrosanct
Legitimate Reference-Point	The Divine (we must, it is sacred)
Motor of Obedience	Faith (fanaticism)
Usual Means of Influence	Preaching
Control of Circulation	Ecclesiastical, Direct (over transmitters)
Status of the Individual	Subject (to be commanded)
Identificatory Myth	Saint
Statement of Personal Authority	God Told Me (Gospel truth)
Regime of Symbolic Authority	The Invisible (the origin) or the unverifiable
Social Unifying Principle	The Symbolic One: the King (dynastic principle)
Subjective Centre of Gravity	Soul (anima)

Printing (Graphosphere)	Audiovisual (Videosphere)
The Sea	Space
Everybody (Nation, People, State) – nationalism and totalitarianism	Each One (population, society, world) – individualism and anomie
Line (history, Progress)	Point (current news, event) – self-centred (the cult of the present)
Adulthood	Youth
Logos (utopias, systems, programmes)	Imago (emotions and fantasies)
Systems (ideologies)	Models (iconology)
Lay Intelligentsia (teachers and doctors) Knowledge is sacrosanct	Media (diffusers and producers) Information is sacrosanct
The Ideal (we must, it is true)	The Performative (we must, it works)
Law (dogmatism)	Public Opinion (relativism)
Publication	Appearance/Broadcasting*
Political, Indirect (over means of transmission)	Economic, Indirect (over messages)
Citizen (to be convinced)	Consumer (to be seduced)
Hero	Star
I Read It In A Book (truth of the printed word)	I Saw it on the TV (truth of the broadcast image)
The Readable (the Foundation) or the logically true	The Visible (the Event) or the apparently true
The Theoretical One: the Leader (ideological principle)	The Arithmetical One: the Leader (statistical principle, opinion poll, rating, audience)
Conscience (animus)	Body (sensorium)

* These terms translate the French '*apparition*', signifying the 'appearance' of something in the public domain (as with the transmission of a television programme or the release of a recording), rather than how it looks.

in which it takes place and to which it gives rise, is subject to the iron law of incompleteness, a law that Michel Serres, in his already cited text on Debray, sees as circular in its application:

> … the history of cultures and societies makes possible an encyclopedic classification of sciences and types of knowledge, whose own history in its turn makes possible sociology, which comes back to culture and history in a vast circle which closes the system and by which the outside and inside feed (upon) each other.[204]

Popper?

This may read less like a statement of incompleteness than like one of a 'hyper-completeness' so comprehensively all- and self-enveloping as to make one wonder about the possibility of any kind of effective intervention in it. The point to be grasped is that none of the parts in Serres's/Debray's circular system is complete in itself, for each defines itself differentially in relation to the others, so that a change in the dominant mode of mediation necessarily entails a change in all the other cultural and ideological phenomena – including the role and definition of culture and ideology themselves – itemised in Debray's table. There are clear traces here of Foucault's notion, in *Les Mots et les choses* (English translation *The Order of Being*), of the *episteme* – the dominant structure of knowing in any period, whose mutations ultimately determine the appearance (and eventual disappearance) of the concept of 'Man'. Foucault, however, does not give the same primacy to material mediation as Debray, and does not mention modern modes of communication. The originality of *Cours de médiologie générale* emerges all the more strikingly when it is placed at the epistemological crossroads I have here attempted to define.

Vie et mort de l'image/Life and Death of the Image (1992) is a sequel or companion-text to *Cours de médiologie générale*. Debray's strength as a mediologist lies largely in his passionate interest in both word and image, both of which (in a move at once rigorously historical and implacably nostalgic) he sees as now overtaken by the visual. 'With the videosphere, we can begin to see the end of the "society of the spectacle" … We were *in the presence of* the image, we are *in* the visual.'[205] The references here are multiple: to the taxonomy of *Cours de médiologie générale*, but also to Guy Debord's Situationist text *La Société du spectacle* (1967), which in a move prophetic of May 1968 denounced late capitalism's systemic relegation of individuals to the role of spectators; to the film critic and writer for *Libération* Serge Daney, whose *Le Salaire du zappeur/The Zapper's Salary* and *Devant la récrudescence des vols de sacs à main* (a reference to the notice warning against thieves in Paris cinemas) are among the first major attempts to engage systematically with the transition from big-screen to television or video film-watching, and back beyond Daney to André Bazin whose stress on the ontology of the visual image (in *Qu'est-ce que le cinéma?/What is Cinema?*) is taken up and reworked in a memorable passage:

> Television shatters the time-honoured device common to theatre, the magic lantern and cinema, which contrasts a dark room with a luminous revelation. The image now incorporates its own light, reveals itself, is thus in our eyes its 'own First Cause' – a Spinozist definition of God or substance. If any projection supposes a projectionist exterior to the screen, and thus a doubling-up, the cathode-ray image fuses the two poles of representation into a kind of emanation of things themselves ... We have moved from an aesthetics to a cosmology.[206]

The function of images, and their decipherment, is thus subject to the same kind of historical determinations and constraints as those of written texts. Ever since 1936 – the year in which Walter Benjamin published *The Work of Art in the Age of Mechanical Reproduction* – it has been all but commonplace to speculate (in both senses) on the demise of the artistic as we know it; Benjamin's observations in many ways prefigure those of Debray ('The mass is a matrix from which all traditional behaviour towards works of art issues today in a new form ... The greatly increased mass of participants has produced a change in the mode of participation').[207] Debray, however, as we might by now expect, adopts a more classificatory, less aphoristic approach. For him, three types of gaze or look – magical, aesthetic and economic – give rise to three regimes of looking – idolatrous, artistic and visual. This might in turn be expected to lead to a table similar to that in *Cours de médiologie générale*, and we are not to be disappointed.

The cinema, in an analysis clearly influenced by the semiotics of Charles Sanders Peirce, has followed a similar historical trajectory from the indexical (the realistic documentary – the Lumière brothers), via the iconic (studio-filmed narrative spectacle – Sternberg, Carné) to the symbolic (film as writing – Godard).[208] What distinguishes Debray's approach from those of more orthodox semioticians (such as Peirce or Christian Metz) is its stress on the role of the image as mediator, which means that 'one cannot take an interest in means of transmission without taking an interest in the religious'.[209] Otherness, incompleteness, the transcendental – these qualities (or are they different names for the same quality?) so important in Debray's later work, are nowhere more so than in his study of the image, which holds a special value (even if a negative one, as with the Muslim prohibition of representations of the Prophet) in virtually all religions:

The Image's …	In the Logosphere (after writing) – Regime of the Idol
Principle of Efficacity (or Relationship to Being)	Presence (transcendental) – the image sees
Mode of Existence	Living (the image is a being)
Crucial Reference (source of authority)	The Supernatural (God)
Source of Light	Spiritual (from within)
Goal and Expectation	Protection (and salvation) – the image captures
Historical Context	From Magic to the Religious (cyclic time)
Ethical Standards	External (theologically and politically governed)
Working Norm and Ideal	I Celebrate (a force) in accordance with the Gospel (the canon)
Time-Span (and working material)	Eternity (repetition) Hard (stone and wood)
Method of Attribution	Collective = Anonymity (from the sorcerer to the artisan)
Producers Organised in …	Clerisy – Corporation
Object of Worship	The Saint (I protect you)
Governing Authority	1: Curial = the Emperor 2: Ecclesiastical = monasteries and cathedrals 3: Noble = the Palace
Continent of Origin and Bridgehead City	Asia – Byzantium (between antiquity and Christianity)
Mode of Accumulation	Public: the Treasury
Aura	Charismatic (anima)
Pathological Tendency	Paranoia
Reach of the Gaze	Through the Image (the visionary goes beyond)
Types of Relationship	Intolerance (religious)

In the Graphosphere (after printing) - Regime of Art	In the Videosphere (after the Audiovisual) – Regime of the Visual
Representation (illusory) – the image is seen	Simulation (digital) – the image is viewed
Physical (the image is a thing)	Virtual (the image is a perception)
The Real (Nature)	The Performing (the machine)
Solar (from without)	Electrical (from within)
Delight (and prestige) – the image captivates	Information (and play/game) – the image is captured
From the Religious to the Historical (linear time)	From the Historical to the Technical (time as succession of events)
Internal (autonomously administered)	Ambient (technico-economically managed)
I Create (a work) in accordance with precedent (the model)	I Produce (an event) in accordance with Myself (the mode)
Immortality (tradition)	The Present Time (innovation)
Flexible (the canvas)	Immaterial (the screen)
Personal = Signature (from the artist to the genius)	Spectacular = logo, brand or designer name (from the entrepreneur to the enterprise)
Academy – School	Network – Profession
The Beautiful (I please you)	The New (I surprise you)
1 : Monarchic = Academic (1500–1750) 2: Bourgeois = Salon + Critics + Gallery (until 1968)	Media/Museums/The Market (plastic arts) Advertising (the audiovisual)
Europe – Florence (between Christianity and modernity)	America – New York (between modern and postmodern)
Private and Individual: collection	Private/Public: reproduction
Pathetic (animus)	Ludic (animation)
Obsession	Schizophrenia
More than the Image (vision contemplates)	Only The Image (viewing controls)
Rivality (Personal)	Competition (economic)

> There is the sacred, in our eyes, wherever the image opens onto something other than itself. The image as denial of the other, even of reality, appears forcefully in the current 'visual' era, which has desacralised the image whilst supposedly consecrating it ... No, everything does not depend on me. There is otherness, which comes before me ... Transcendence simply means exteriority – not what is beyond, but what lies outside.[210]

What this means (to oversimplify) is that the sacred – 'a rational, secular word, despite its bad reputation with agnostics'[211] – has no necessary connection with organised religion or belief/disbelief in (a) God; it is an anthropological function common to any human grouping (much as the Other, for thinkers as at least apparently dissimilar as Sartre and Lacan, is a structurally necessary component of any human sense of identity), and can be disregarded only at one's peril. This is what underpins the seemingly oxymoronic assertion that 'a WYSIWYG – "what you see is what you get" – society is no longer an open society', for its very permeability and fluidity – its 'openness' in one sense – deprive it of its opening onto otherness and the outside. 'The recorded image reinforces the authority of the event with the terrorism of evidence';[212] here again it is unclear – perhaps at this stage unknowable? – whether Debray is analytically accounting for the inevitable erosion of the imagination by the image, or lodging a romantic protest against it. His concluding paragraph enacts the constitutive ambiguity of his position:

> The mediologist is banned from moralising ... His task, within the limits set by objective research, is to describe and to try to explain. His ambition from now on, when he emerges from the boundaries of his discipline, will be to plead for the invisible.[213]

Between the detached analyst and the concerned individual, the role or persona that seems to have slipped away here is that of the committed intellectual – for Debray, of course, quintessentially a construct of the graphosphere, yet one that almost in spite of himself continues to inhabit his work. No better proof of this could be required than the conclusion of his next book, *L'État séducteur/The Seducer State* (1993), which after a ruthless dissection of how the French state has been undermined by the audiovisual era ends with a rousing call for 'Less physics, please, and a little more metaphysics! We are stifling! Break down the walls of images, reopen with words the windows of the wide open sea!'[214] This sounds poetic rather than *engagé*, but perhaps that is what *engagement*, in the age of the videosphere, will necessarily sound like; and Debray's previous paragraph has made it plain that any and every human *polis* is reliant on the performative absence characteristic, I would argue, as much of poetry as it is of religion or even of politics:

> Man is the only animal fulfilled only by absence, which makes him a genuinely political animal who will never be fulfilled by the economy alone. Christ satisfied us for so long because he is the radically absent one, proclaimed by the angel to be not here but elsewhere. His tomb would not have galvanised people's imaginations had it not been empty. His body: a word. Now that it is no longer the spokesperson for the nation or the defender of the people, the state no longer speaks to us, or rather it no longer speaks to us of the nation and the people – its *raisons d'être* – but merely of itself. The means has supplanted the end.[215]

The themes here – the centrality of the nation and of defence, the performative force of (the) word(s), the inescapability of incompleteness – will be familiar from Debray's other work. What *L'État séducteur* does is to give them a pungent polemical relevance to the France of the early 1990s, hinted at in its contrast between 'so-called right-wing governments mentally dominated by the myths of the left (de Gaulle) and the opposite (Mitterrand)'.[216] This too is what it might be best to call *déjà lu*, but now Debray's mediological analysis provides a trenchant theoretical framework for his strictures on the corruption (the word is not too strong) of the nation state by the all-showingness of the audiovisual image. 'In a videocracy, (physical) personalisation tends to ruin (moral) personification. Transparency liquidates transcendence.'[217] Bill Clinton photographed jogging before expatiating on the desirability of the electronic referendum, or the heir to the British throne ruefully admitting live on television the adultery enthusiastically practised by so many of his predecessors without bringing the monarchic institution into jeopardy, are vivid contemporary examples of the manner in which the all-pervasive concreteness of the videosphere has corroded the abstraction – the incompleteness – indispensable to any social formation.

Paradoxically, and at the same time, it has also been responsible for what might be termed (the expression is mine, not Debray's) a 'false', or 'weak', abstraction. The manner in which television cameras have brought images of suffering in the Third World into Western living-rooms may have led to much beneficent reaching for cheque-books, but at the cost of an understanding of the particularity of each situation. 'The indexical image in its raw state carries no geographical or chronological information ... The visual sphere speaks every language *because it speaks none*.'[218] The glutinous, and intellectually lazy, generalities of 'human rights' stand in stark contrast to the historical and geographical specificities of each continent, each nation-state, each contending group. Because the videosphere is characterised by 'weak information and strong communication',[219] its rise is intimately connected – at least as much so as the waning of Marxism as a geopolitical force – with the pervasive sense that Third World 'tragedies' are somehow structurally inevitable, and can be alleviated only at the level of the individual. People can help, but citizens are powerless.

Debray also criticises the contemporary (for which read post-1968) perversion of the ideal of the festival or celebration (the French *fête* connotes both of these as well as in a Bakhtinian sense 'carnival').* 'Festival satisfies the unconscious desire of any community',[220] and is thus one of the major institutions in and through which incompleteness asserts itself; but the contemporary festival – Jack Lang and the bicentennial both clearly in Debray's sights though not overtly alluded to – is no longer 'the Celebration of a lost origin; it has become a self-sufficient, self-referential Event'.[221] Festival, that is to say, has lost the abstract, absent, conceptual component that gave it its real dignity and importance.

So too has the (French) state, and it is in the preface to *L'État séducteur* that Debray justifies his decision to leave the Conseil d'État, since 'it was easier to resist the new natural law of omnipresent market and omnipresent community by ceasing to hold an official position once the state demagogically resigned itself to the way things were'.[222] That resignation has entailed the decline of the 'educating state' and the rise of the 'seducer State',[223] traced in a provocative move reminiscent of *Modeste contribution* back to the misbegotten heritage of 1968:

> The denunciation of 'bourgeois education', full of good intentions as it was, has helped to make commercialised education acceptable twenty years on ... It is not out of the question that the theoretical leftism of the 1960s and 1970s – unwillingly, of course – in some measure contributed to the widespread acceptance of the practical or vocational reaction of the 1980s and 1990s.

When Debray goes on to say that 'schools no longer have *pupils* nor universities *students* (with the discipline and obligations those words imply), but *users* like public transport, and soon no doubt *customers* like Air France',[224] those involved with the increasingly commercialised world of British and US education may well feel a twinge of recognition. The post-1968 'delegitimisation of closed

* 'Carnival is a pageant without footlights and without a division into performers and spectators. In carnival everyone is an active participant, everyone communes in the carnival act' – Mikhail Bakhtin, *Problems of Dostoevsky's Poetics* (Manchester, Manchester University Press, 1984), p.122

education in the name of an open society and of knowledge in the name of life'[225] has led – by only one of its necessarily multifarious routes, but by one that the increasing dominance of privatised culture and market economics has made far more important than could have been foreseen at the time – to a vocationalisation ('training for "life"') and an atomising decentralisation ('in the name of an open society') that run counter to the state educational values Debray holds so dear. Education is 'no longer a historic mission but one insoluble social problem among others (law and order, unemployment, the budget deficit)'[226] – as severe a criticism of a decade of Socialist rule as it would be possible to conceive, and beyond that – for *L'État séducteur* is philosophy as well as polemic – an observation with incalculably grave implications for the future of the (not only French) nation-state. If mediology, as Debray states in his preface, 'can be defined as the ecology of cultural systems',[227] then the changes in the communicative environment of the state – changes which it has colluded with and even encouraged – may well prove fatal to its cultural and political system. For one who 'regards the existence of a unitary, centralised state as the worst of all evils except for whatever may come after it',[228] this is a grave prognosis indeed.

This is the last of Debray's books (to date) to engage explicitly with developments in contemporary France. His 'vow of political silence' in *Les Empires contre l'Europe* could in one albeit narrow sense be said to have remained inviolate, since neither his 'Gaullist-republican' nor his mediological work contains any overt programmatic political exhortations or injunctions. We have, however, seen that it is quite impossible to avoid reading these texts as a fiercely plangent indictment of the France of Mitterrand's second term. 'Political' in the narrower sense this may not be, for there is little feeling that an alternative ideology or even programme might bring about an improvement; but it has seldom seemed truer than for Debray that the withdrawal from the political is itself a kind of political act.

So, too, it must have been for Pierre Bérégovoy, last to date of France's Socialist prime ministers, whose suicide on 1 May 1993 was widely interpreted as a protest against his sidelining by Mitterrand after the crushing electoral defeat of the previous month. *Un mot encore, cher Béré/Just One Word More, Dear 'Béré'* is a short pamphlet written by Debray one week after the suicide. Bérégovoy was a Gas Board employee who worked his way up through the political and trade union ranks, and a seasoned intriguer – a figure about as far removed from Debray's intellectual urbanity as could be imagined. 'We didn't really like each other. My invincible repulsion for the trade-union *apparatchik* no doubt corresponded to your scorn, half-amused half-fearful, for phrasemongers.'[229]

Debray nevertheless salutes Bérégovoy's courage in brutally acknowledging his betrayal of the class from which he came, whilst resisting the hagiographisation that followed immediately on his death ('the distance is too great between the martyr to an ideal and the professional and only very moderately idealistic politician I knew').[230] The fact that he did not leave so much as a note is seen as 'a lesson in professional morality – a state lesson',[231] and we may be reminded of Debray's admiration for de Gaulle's wish that no statues should be erected of him after his death. Bérégovoy 'reminds us that when there used to be a state, respect for oneself and others imposed a "duty of reserve"'.[232]

Debray declares his continuing loyalty to the principles of 1981 ('that wonderful moment of naivety'),[233] though he considers it still too early to pronounce on 'the three medals of that decade' – 'the abolition of the death penalty, the brief return of civic education in schools and the foundation of Arte [France's alternative television channel]'.[234] For these, Bérégovoy's persistence and tenacity deserve their share of credit; if 'at least nobody will say that everything between 1981 and 1993 was simply derisory', that is because of his suicide in defence of his honour rather than in spite of it. Yet 'the humanitarian struggles of those who want to change the way people live have far less influence than the technical inventions of those who just wanted to improve this or that little machine (and thereby changed the world)'.[235] The overwhelming of politics by the videosphere here comes perilously close to simple technological determinism, and Debray's admiration for Bérégovoy reads like an epitaph for an entire species of *homme d'État* rather than for one member of it.

His most recent mediological text (at the time of writing), *Manifestes médiologiques/Mediological Manifestos* (1994), is in fact a juxtaposition of two texts, each produced with a specific academic aim in mind. *Défendre l'image/In Defence of the Image* (here reproduced second) was presented orally at the Sorbonne on 23 October 1993, in support of Debray's request to be awarded the degree of Doctor of Philosophy for *Vie et mort de l'image*. The more substantial *Pour une médiologie/Towards (in Favour of) a Mediology* was likewise presented on 8 January 1994 to earn him 'qualification to direct research'. Both submissions were granted – the second, at which I was present, after a nearly six-hour viva, which in France always takes the form of a public debate or *disputatio* between candidate and jury. This return to the academy of an eminent 'prodigal son' is an entirely consequent one, for we have just seen that for Debray the State education system is at once an intellectually necessary and a culturally beleaguered institution. What better way of helping to resolve this paradox than to return to that institution armed with an academically rigorous disciplinary framework for understanding the very conditions of its jeopardy?

Défendre l'image makes fully explicit for the first time Debray's relationship to semiology (Eco, Peirce, Barthes are all cited as pretexts), without which mediology would clearly have been unthinkable but which is criticised for 'finding at the end of [its] analyses only what had been put in at the beginning',[236] and more seriously for its desire to tame and reappropriate the image in the name of the Word:

> Perhaps the man of words feels vaguely guilty faced with transmission without words and signs without a code. Perhaps we could interpret the semiological vogue and all its ways of verbalising the non-verbal as a return to sender, a ruse to throw suspicion on all those loudmouths who escape the order of the code. Perhaps there is behind these learned attempts to tame madcap imagination with verbal reason ... a refusal to accept the fundamental non-intelligibility of the image, its resistance to and checkmating of Logos.[237]

Debray's own work would doubtless claim to escape such criticism, since he does not so much analyse or decode images as situate historically and contextually the period of their hegemony. Where the image, on this account, resists the (would-be) all-explicitatory reach of Logos is in its constitutive incompleteness, since any image is of something or somebody who is not or no longer there, and in that sense at least partakes of the religious. 'The question: "why are there images rather than nothing?" has for a long time had a plausible answer: "Because man is the only animal who knows himself to be mortal."'[238]

Pour une médiologie continues to develop 'the religious syntax of collective life',[239] once again with reference to the theorem of Gödel (see p. 26). Here Debray emphasises that he is not an analyst of 'the media' in the conventional sense – there is little sustained reference in his work to this journal or that television programme, at any rate once we get past *Le Pouvoir intellectuel en France* – but that his point of view is a longer-term one, in which 'the moment is understood through the process as the part is through the whole'.[240] *Le Pouvoir intellectuel* is seen retroactively as the unconscious starting-point of Debray's mediological enterprise, foregrounding as it did, not 'a substantive definition of the "intellectual" as the "person of ideas and values"', but 'an operational definition as "the person of transmission" (of ideas and values)'. This has made possible a positional – not to say functionalist – analysis in which the role of the media today is seen as literally identical to that of the clergy in earlier times ('The working journalist ... is the parish priest; the chief editor an archbishop; the 8 p.m.

broadcaster, with jurisdiction over the entire country, the Primate of France'.)[241]

The most often-cited contemporary equivalent to the clergy is the therapeutic and psychoanalytic profession. For Debray, this comparison is valid in that where once the exhortation to give to the poor came from the pulpit, now it comes from the television screen. The strictures on semiology found in *Défendre l'image* recur here, with their stress on the material and sensory fabric of the non-verbal text. 'Exclusive insistence upon language has turned human sciences into half-human sciences, like a person with one leg or a brain missing one hemisphere.'[242] This evokes Leroi-Gourhan's work (*Le geste et la Parole/Gesture and Language*; *L'Homme et la matière/Mankind and Matter*), and also in some ways the emphasis placed by Bourdieu (nowhere mentioned, curiously, in Debray) upon the importance of the bodily *habitus* and other non-linguistic factors, if only to the extent that it inscribes itself within a sustained theoretical and analytic challenge to the (erstwhile?) hegemony of structuralism and semiology.

That challenge has also to do with semiology's 'satellisation of sense around a ruling consciousness',[243] and concomitant under-estimation of the force of technological systems. Mediology, on the other hand, is so far from claiming any kind of phenomenological detachment that as we have intermittently seen it may run the risk of self-deconstructive fatalism. 'Mediologists do not cohabit with their technical milieu, they are inhabited by their habitat – constructed by the niche they themselves construct.'[244] This aporia is not dissimilar to that faced by structuralists confronting the omnipresence and inescapability of language, from which post-structuralism or deconstruction (however, within reason, defined) were strategies for extracting themselves. Debray calls upon what might almost literally be described as a *deus ex machina* to slip the bonds of technical determinism. Machines will never dominate us because we must die:

> Machines have been models for thinking, yesterday, about the body (Descartes), and today, in the computer era, for thinking about intelligence (Turing). They will never be able to be models for thinking about thought, for the ultimate reason that machines are not mortal and only a mortal being can accede to the symbolic universe of values and meanings. Death, at once anticipated and deferred by our technical grasp of the world, is also that which it cannot overcome. Awareness of mortality, the driving motor of technical development, remains the irreducible interiority of human beings.[245]

The movement beyond the technological to the religious (not, let us remember, to be equated with 'religion') is that from the illusion of completeness to the knowledge of incompleteness – a Sisyphean knowledge, readers of Camus will undoubtedly observe, but one that here serves to provoke less a metaphysics of stoicism than a vehement concluding exhortation to 'transform our culture into an organised offensive of memory ... [and] to reinscribe with euphoric stubbornness earlier legacies into new productions of the unknown'.[246] Uttered in the Sorbonne, at the heart of the French educational system, this clearly goes beyond an individual assertion of project and purpose to become a call for the founding and institutionalisation of a new discipline.

Debray's most recent book (at the time of writing) is *L'Oeil naïf/The Innocent Eye* (1994). This is presented in the introduction as a kind of *divertissement* ('I have left behind the cumbersome baggage of the mediologist to make my way as lightly and openly as possible'), encouraged by the medium with which it deals ('Photography is an invitation to play truant').[247] Playing truant from the discipline of mediology does not, however, mean forgetting all its precepts. Debray makes it plain that he is not so much decoding the images he has chosen – the semiological project criticised in *Manifestes médiologiques* – as engaging with their unspeaking resistance ('What fascinates me in the long run in an image is everything in it that blocks words, its incommunicability ... To speak a silence – there is a wager that puts one to the test').[248] His attachment to photography is linked to its artisanal status, contrasted with the industry of the moving image, and his work on it is defined in unabashedly personal, emotional terms:

> No prejudices, no pretensions. Not a semiological dismantling (enough of decoding!), nor an ideological demystification (enough of suspicion!), but a wonderment trying to understand itself, an excitement giving its reasons in the first person, without a song and dance.[249]

This 'first-person' quality, which in a sense assimilates *L'Oeil naïf* as much to *Les Masques* as to the more theoretical mediological work, yields a text that was for me (the first person is catching) a sheer delight to read. The account of it I shall give here is of necessity an arbitrary and personal one, concentrating on those among the twenty-five main photographs in the book that most touched or interested me. Robert Doisneau's *Le Baiser de l'Hôtel de Ville* – probably the most famous French photograph ever – is taken to task as a 'stereotyped image of Paris that overencodes eternal Parisian qualities', and exudes 'a suspicion of benign Pétainism, anarchistic and vaguely of the Left'.[250] The expression '*Typically french* [sic]'[251] is even used in English to deflate the photograph's citational, quite literally *déjà vu* quality – not an uncourageous thing to do given its hardy mythical status as representative of dear-old-black-and-white Paris.

More serious by half is an unattributed photo taken in the Quartier du Temple (a Jewish area) in 1941, depicting a crowd idly watching a busload of Jews being driven off to the camps. Debray moves beyond horrified fascination with the banality of the image ('That day ... the French version of the Final Solution was this gathering of passers-by around a minor news story'),[252] to reflect that up until the Liberation 'the Resistance exists for us through texts and Collaboration through photographs'.[253] Given that the Resistance was necessarily clandestine this is perhaps not surprising, but it provides a valuable framework to think about the traumatic impact made by Marcel Ophuls's 1969 documentary film *Le Chagrin et la Pitié/The Sorrow and the Pity*, whose images – 'a mythological catastrophe'[254] – irrevocably shook the hegemony of the Resistance myth. It is difficult not to map onto this duality of word and image Debray's own leaning, for all his love of the image, towards a culture of the word. If literary Resistance and visual Collaboration 'struggle in French memories as image and text do in our culture',[255] is this not a further indication – perhaps an ultimate one – that politically and even ethically right is on the side of the text?

The essay commentating on Charles Marville's 1865 photograph of the Place Saint-André-des-Arts, entitled *Les murs muent* – at once 'walls change' and a pun on *murmures*/'murmurs' – brings out the photograph's spectral quality (it was taken in the very early morning when nobody was about), and stresses in tones reminiscent of Walter Benjamin the propaedeutic, educational role of photography, which:

> ... can correct my drifting eye and make me a meticulous *flâneur* ... who will set off to the baker's shop inspecting carvings and door-surrounds, and walk down his street each day for the ten thousandth time as though he were seeing it for the first time.[256]

Immediately beneath this paragraph we find an 1866 Marville photograph of the Rue de l'Odéon, on the Left Bank – the street in which Debray lives, as though to reinforce the work's private, autobiographical quality ... New York, in the following essay, is contrasted with Paris as the great cinematic as opposed to literary mythical city, and the implied obsolescence of Paris underscored by Seb Janiak's untitled colour photograph (in *Effet spécial/Special Effect*) of Notre-Dame in ruins overgrown with lush tropical vegetation. It is the 'melancholy of the future'[257] that Debray finds at work in Janiak's computer-produced 'reconstruction' of, precisely, a future so far off as to be humanly inconceivable.

Debray's political antecedents reveal themselves clearly in the following text, *Le portrait du roi/The Portrait of the King* – an analysis (more of a 'decoding' in the classical sense than the other texts discussed) of the official photographs taken of each of the four presidents of the Fifth Republic shortly after their election. There is a clear break between those of de Gaulle and Pompidou, in full ceremonial dress, and Giscard, wearing a lounge suit and photographed against a slanting tricolour background to show that he 'understood the new deal that came out of May 1968'.[258] Mitterrand's choice of the émigré German photographer Gisèle Freund – a friend of Walter Benjamin's and active in the Popular Front – is seen as significant, 'a fine fantasy ... about making the "socialist-communist" government the good-natured continuation of the Popular Front'.[259] No less so is Mitterrand's literary background – quite literally, photographed as he is with a bookcase full of leather-bound tomes behind him and a volume of Montaigne's *Essais* in his hand. Debray clearly finds attractive – it would be difficult not to – the juxtaposition of literary culture and old-fashioned peasant sensuality ('the gilded richness of ... the bookshelves and bindings, leather, paper, wood').[260] Those who read *L'Oeil naïf* with a less innocent eye may, however, find themselves troubled by the recollection of an earlier photograph, reproduced in the essay on the Occupation (*Circulez, il n'y a rien à voir/Move on, There's Nothing to See*) – of René Bousquet, in charge of police under the Occupation, who it was revealed almost as Debray's book was published had been on friendly terms with Mitterrand until a few years before his assassination in 1992 ... There can be few better illustrations of how dependent photographs are on an ever-changing context.

Cuba figures in *Histoire ancienne/Ancient History*, where Roger Pic's photograph of Revolution Square in Havana in 1962 is lauded because it depicts 'the crowd ... for itself, as the central and principal subject'.[261] Castro's absence from the photograph is what gives it its continuing power to stir, placing collective enthusiasm rather than its object at the centre. Contemporary humanitarian photography, on the other hand, is roundly denounced (in *Le porno humanitaire/Humanitarian Porn*), in an argument sufficiently similar to that of *L'État séducteur* not to need rehearsing here.

The text closes on two essays each in its own way permeated by the divine and its absence. *Ex-voto* juxtaposes photographs of Orson Welles and de Gaulle to show that 'the two men of this century I admire most, and for whom 1940 was their best year (*Citizen Kane* is a contemporary of de Gaulle's 18 June broadcast), have a certain resemblance'.[262] Debray's keeping always in his desk 'relics' of Welles and the General is, as we might expect, presented as an instance of the universal human need to link oneself to one's community with signs and icons, and there is a not unpleasing one-upmanship in his preference for 'my domestic Pantheon' to the 'giants with feet of clay'[263] – Tapie and Berlusconi, as we might expect, but also the Pope – promoted by the television image.

In *Le Tombeau vide et après/The Empty Tomb and Afterwards*, Debray speaks of his response to the news that the Shroud of Turin had been scientifically shown to be a fabrication – 'good news, presaging as it did long preparatory work and a kind of appeal to mobilise the shadows within'.[264] This is because it affirms the priority of icons over indices, of the humanly-created image over the optical miracle, and thus of the reality of illusion over the illusion of reality. 'Photography too is an idol, let us not believe blindly in it; real presences are elsewhere.'[265] That 'elsewhere,' in its changing, historically determined and determinant complexity, is what Debray's work on the image and on mediology sets itself the task of exploring.

Conclusion

To conclude so brief a survey of a thinker whose work is not merely still in progress, but at what is likely to prove a determinant conceptual and institutional crossroads, is almost an absurd task. Perhaps I should either simply have stopped where the published work (at the time of writing) does, or allowed myself a provocatively lame pun on the necessity of incompleteness and tiptoed coyly off-stage. This would, however, have been to fail in my duty to provide an answer to the question the book overall poses – why Debray's work is in my judgement not merely of interest, but (even where I disagree with him) of a much greater importance for understanding the contemporary world than seems to be generally recognised.

There are, of course, many answers to this, even disregarding the obvious – and thereby obtrusive – fascination with his adventurous early career. I do not share, as will doubtless have been obvious, his scepticism about politics as a sphere for effective social action. Nor, on the other hand, do I share, perhaps mercifully, his experience of long and fatiguing political action in a country which for fourteen years had a Socialist head of state. *Tout comprendre, c'est tout pardonner*? Maybe; but beyond this what I find interesting, because original, is Debray's analysis of the undoubted large-scale failures (along with a number of major successes) of the French Socialists. That analysis is grounded neither in a ('left') rhetoric of betrayal, nor in a ('right') stigmatisation of irrelevance and wrong-headedness, but in an engagement with the realities of cultural change that lends it genuine depth.

That engagement in turn leads to two other reasons why I am convinced of the importance of Debray's work. One is its recognition of the indispensability of incompleteness to human social organisation and, consequently, of that of word and image – from the Christian sacraments to Jacques Derrida, both signs of an 'absent presence'. This makes possible a historicisation of culture which recognises the vast changes that are still taking place without the otiose, giggling rush to embrace them characteristic of so much second division postmodernism. It is still much too early to pronounce on the future of mediology as a discipline (that will depend, among other things, precisely on politically-motivated decisions ...), but it has the potential to become extremely significant, not least in providing a conduit between work in media studies and the more arrogantly established disciplines of history and philosophy.

The other reason can be given in two words: 'Silvio Berlusconi'. That individual's exemplary career is as vivid an illustration of Debray's mediological theses as could be imagined. The primacy of the 'mediatic' over the ideological; the meretricious hegemony of the 'spectacle' (Debord) or the 'hyperreal' (Baudrillard), and the corresponding devaluation of words and argument; the promiscuous melding of wildly divergent elements into a coalition whose members were brought together only by their exclusion from previous apparatuses of state power; above all, perhaps, the folly of imagining that a terminally corrupt state could ever be bailed out by a civil society that had somehow remained immune to its contagion – confronted with these it would be tempting, if/because monumentally unfair, to ascribe to Debray the reflection that 'if Berlusconi did not exist, it would be necessary to invent him'. The conceptual weight and long-term historical seriousness of Debray's thought reinforce, rather than detract from, its contribution to an understanding of a world in which Forza Italia and 'human rights' could seriously be promoted as the *nec plus ultra* of humankind as it enters the twenty-first century.

References

1. For consideration of the debates this aroused around the bicentennial celebrations of 1989, see Sunil Khilnani, *Arguing Revolution: The Intellectual Left in Postwar France* (New Haven and London: Yale University Press, 1993), particularly pp.155–78.
2. For more detailed information on this see Pascal Ory and Jean-François Sirinelli, *Les Intellectuels en France, de l'Affaire Dreyfus à nos jours* (Paris: Armand Colin, 1986), pp.15–16.
3. Ed. Anne Fremantle, *Mao Tse-Tung: An Anthology of his Writings* (New York and Scarborough, Ontario: New American Library, 1971), p.240.
4. This essay, first published in 1962, is contained in Louis Althusser, *Pour Marx* (Paris: Maspéro, 1971), pp.87–128. The essays brought together in this volume all formed part of Althusser's attempt at producing a new, properly 'scientific' reading of Marx.
5. V.I. Lenin, *What is to be Done?* (Moscow: Progress Publishers, 1947), p.31.
6. Régis Debray (trans. R. Sheed), *Prison Writings* (New York: Random House, 1973), p.200.
7. Hartmut Ramon, *The Marxism of Régis Debray: Between Lenin and Guevara* (Lawrence: Regents Press of Kansas, 1978), p.4.
8. Ernesto 'Che' Guevara, *Socialism and Man in Cuba* (Sydney: Pathfinder/Pacific and Asia, 1988), p.13.
9. Mao Tse-Tung and Che Guevara, *Guerrilla Warfare* (London: Cassell, 1962), p.111.
10. Guevara, *Guerrilla Warfare*, p.120.
11. Ibid p.156.
12. Régis Debray (ed. Robin Blackburn), *Strategy for Revolution* (London: Jonathan Cape, 1970), p.27.
13. V.I. Lenin. *State and Revolution*, in Arthur P. Mendel (ed.), *Essential Works of Marxism* (New York: Bantam Books, 1961), p.129.
14. Khilnani, *Arguing Revolution*; Ory and Sirinelli, *Les Intellectuels en France*; and Keith A. Reader, *Intellectuals and the Left in France since 1968* (London: Macmillan, 1987) all provide valuable contextualising information and analysis here.

15. Debray, *Strategy for Revolution*, p.81.
16. Ibid., p.80.
17. Ibid., p.81.
18. Ibid., p.116.
19. Ibid., pp.123–4.
20. Ibid., p.139.
21. Ibid.
22. Ibid., p.147.
23. Ibid., p.152.
24. Ramon, *The Marxism of Régis Debray*, p.196.
25. Debray, *Strategy for Revolution*, p.158.
26. Ibid., p.159.
27. Ibid.
28. Régis Debray (trans. Bobbye Ortiz), *Revolution in the Revolution?* (Harmondsworth: Penguin, 1967), p.11.
29. Foreword to Debray, *Revolution in the Revolution?*, p.10.
30. Edgar Morin (with Claude Lefort and Cornelius Castoriadis), *Mai 68: La Brèche suivi de Vingt Ans Après* (Paris: Éditions Complexe, 1988), p.181.
31. Debray, *Revolution in the Revolution?*, p.21.
32. Ibid., p.26.
33. Ibid., p.36.
34. V. Henri Lefebvre, *L'Idéologie structuraliste* (Paris: Points, 1975).
35. Debray, *Revolution in the Revolution?*,p.39.
36. Ibid., p.38.
37. Ibid., p.59.
38. Ibid., p.64.
39. Ibid., p.68.
40. Ibid., p.82.
41. Karl Marx, 'Preface to *A Contribution to the Critique of Political Economy*', in Marx and Engels, *Selected Works* (Moscow: Progress Publishers, 1973), Vol.I, p.503.
42. Leo Huberman and Paul M. Sweezy (eds), *Régis Debray and the Latin American Revolution* (New York: Monthly Review Press, 1968), p.4.
43. Debray, *Revoluton in the Revolution?*, pp.96–7.
44. Ibid., p.105.
45. Ibid., p.108
46. Ibid., pp.108–9.
47. Ibid., p.111.
48. Ibid., p.127.
49. Debray, *Strategy for Revolution*, pp.200–1.
50. Eqbal Ahmad, 'Radical But Wrong', in Huberman and Sweezy (eds), *Régis Debray and the Latin American Revolution*, p.82.

51. Ramon, *The Marxism of Régis Debray*, p.37.
52. In Régis Debray, *La Critique des armes* (Paris: Seuil, 1974), p.264.
53. Debray, *Strategy for Revolution*, p.236.
54. Régis Debray (trans. Rosemary Sheed), *Prison Writings* (London: Allen Lane, 1973), p.186.
55. Ibid., p.189.
56. Ibid., p.205.
57. Ibid., p.102.
58. Ibid., p.106.
59. *Politique-Hebdo*, 1 July 1973, p.11.
60. Régis Debray, *Entretiens avec Allende sur la situation au Chili* (Paris: Maspéro, 1971), p.48.
61. Debray, *Entretiens avec Allende*, p.137.
62. Ibid., p.130. (Cf. *Carrillo – demain l'Espagne* – interviews with the Spanish Communist leader by Debray and Max Gallo – Paris: Seuil, 1974).
63. Régis Debray, *La Critique des armes* (Paris: Seuil, 1974), p.36.
64. Régis Debray, *La Guerrilla du Che* (Paris: Seuil, 1974), p.174.
65. Régis Debray, *L'Indésirable* (Paris: Seuil, 1975), p.189.
66. Ibid., p.25.
67. Ibid., p.220.
68. Régis Debray, *La Neige brûle* (Paris: Grasset, 1977), p.281.
69. Ibid., p.115.
70. Ibid., p.35.
71. Ibid., p.143.
72. Ibid., p.194.
73. Ibid., p.209.
74. For more information on this movement see Keith A. Reader, *Intellectuals and the Left in France since 1968* (London: Macmillan, 1987), and François Aubral and Xavier Delcourt, *Contre la nouvelle philosophie* (Paris: Gallimard, 1977).
75. Debray, *La Neige brûle*, p.210.
76. Régis Debray, *Journal d'un petit bourgeois entre deux feux et quatre murs* (Paris: Seuil, 1976), p.73.
77. Régis Debray, *Les Masques* (Paris: Gallimard, 1987), pp.124–6.
78. Ibid., p.103.
79. Régis Debray, *Les Rendez-Vous Manqués* (Paris: Seuil, 1975), p.113.
80. Ibid., p.128.
81. See Keith A. Reader, *Intellectuals and the Left in France since 1968* for a more detailed exposition of this.
82. Debray, *Les Rendez-Vous Manqués*, p.156.

83. Ibid., p.147. ('Great day' here translates 'le Grand Soir' – the moment when in revolutionary mythology the passage from the old to the new social order is accomplished.)
84. Régis Debray, *Modeste contribution aux discours et cérémonies officielles du dixième anniversaire* (Paris: François Maspero, 1978), p.10. (For a comprehensive overview of the other kinds of interpretation of May 1968 that have been proferred at different times, see Keith A. Reader, *The May 1968 Events in France*, London: Macmillan, 1993.)
85. Debray, *Modeste contribution* , p.12.
86. For further analysis of this see Keith A. Reader, *The May 1968 Events in France*, notably chapter 4.
87. Debray, *Modeste contribution* , p.89.
88. Ibid., p.68.
89. Ibid., p.87.
90. Régis Debray, *Lettres aux communistes français et à quelques autres* (Paris: Seuil, 1978), pp.7–8.
91. Michel de Certeau, *La prise de parole* (Paris: Seuil, 1994), p.40.
92. Debray, *Lettres aux communistes français*, p.28.
93. Ibid., p.132.
94. Régis Debray and Jean Ziegler, *Il s'agit de ne pas se rendre* (Paris: Arléa, 1994), p.29.
95. Régis Debray, *Le Pouvoir intellectuel en France* (Paris: Ramsay, 1979), p.8.
96. Ibid., p.57.
97. Ibid., p.184.
98. Ibid., p.252.
99. Ibid., p.251.
100. Ibid., p.22.
101 Ibid., p.28.
102. Priscilla Parkhurst Clark, *Literary France: The Making of a Culture* (Berkeley: University of California Press, 1991), p.218.
103. Debray, *Le Pouvoir intellectuel en France*, p.133.
104. Ibid., p.277.
105. Ibid., p.129.
106. See Pascal Ory and Jean-François Sirinelli, *Les Intellectuels en France, de l'affaire Dreyfus à nos jours* (Paris: 1986), for a detailed historical coverage of this.
107. Régis Debray, *Le Scribe* (Paris: Grasset, 1980), p.68.
108. Ibid., p.130.
109. Ibid., p.45.
110. Ibid., p.65.
111. Ibid., p.67.
112. Ibid., p.140.
113. Clark, *Literary France*, p.159.

114. Debray, *Le Scribe*, p.151.
115. Ibid., p.156.
116. Ibid., p.158.
117. Ibid., p.170.
118. Ibid., p.230.
119. Ibid., p.242.
120. Ibid., p.268.
121. Ibid., p.300.
122. Régis Debray, *Critique de la raison politique* (Paris: Gallimard, 1981), pp.20–2.
123. Ibid., p.30.
124. Ibid., p.39. (The French has 'ont mal à la nation', which implies a simultaneous difficulty and suffering or pain not readily capturable in English.)
125. Ibid., p.43.
126. Ibid., p.30.
127. Ibid., p.56.
128. Ibid., p.70.
129. Ibid., p.117.
130. Ibid., p.161.
131. Ibid., p.180.
132. Ibid., p.257.
133. Michel Serres (ed.), *Éléments d'histoire des sciences* (Paris, Bordas: 1989), p.358.
134. Debray, *Critique de la raison politique*, p.461.
135. Ibid., p.468.
136. Régis Debray, *La Puissance et les rêves* (Paris: Gallimard, 1984), p.96.
137. Ibid., p.52.
138. Ibid., p.38.
139. Ibid., p.72.
140. Ibid., p.89.
141. Ibid., p.120.
142. Ibid., p.237.
143. Ibid., p.258.
144. Ibid., pp.303–4.
145. Régis Debray, *Les Empires contre l'europe* (Paris: Gallimard, 1985), pp.20–1.
146. Ibid., p.58.
147. Ibid., p.119.
148. Ibid., p.247.
149. Ibid., p.167.
150. Ibid., p.336.
151. Ibid., p.345.
152. Ibid., p.344.
153. Ibid., p.346.

154. Ibid., p.180.
155. Régis Debray, *Tous azimuts* (Paris: Éditions Odile Jacob, 1989), p.9.
156. Ibid., p.11.
157. Ibid., p.38.
158. Ibid., p.83.
159. Ibid., p.87.
160. Ibid., p.132.
161. Régis Debray, *Éloges* (Paris: Gallimard, 1986), p.122.
162. Régis Debray, *Comète, ma comète* (Paris: Gallimard, 1986), p.67.
163. Ibid., p.81.
164. Ibid., p.138.
165. For more extended treatment of this see my chapter in Jill Forbes and Mike Kelly (eds.), *French Cultural Studies: an Introduction* (Oxford: Oxford University Press, forthcoming).
166. Ibid.
167. Régis Debray, *Les Masques* (Paris: Gallimard, 1987), p.15.
168. Ibid., p.169.
169. Ibid., p.93.
170. Ibid., p.139.
171. Ibid., p.42.
172. Ibid., p.15.
173. Ibid., p.257.
174. Ibid., p.219.
175. Ibid., p.220.
176. Régis Debray, *Contretemps: éloges des idéaux perdus* (Paris: Gallimard/Folio, 1992), p.79.
177. Debray, *Le Pouvoir intellectuel en France*, p.22.
178. Georg Lukács, *Studies in European Realism* (London: Merlin Press, 1972), p.10.
179. Debray, *Contretemps*, p.15.
180. Ibid., p.16.
181. Régis Debray, *Que vive la République!* (Paris: Odile Jacob, 1989), p.58.
182. Ibid., p.18. (The capital letters, giving the institutions in question something of the status of Balzacian personified abstractions, reproduce those in Debray's French text.)
183. Ibid., p.110.
184. Ibid., p.111.
185. Ibid., p.57.
186. Ibid., p.180.
187. Ibid., p.141.
188. Régis Debray, *A demain de Gaulle!* (Paris: Gallimard/Le Débat, 1990), p.33.

189. Ibid., p.39. ('Memories and memoirs' here translates the French 'Mémoires', which bears both senses.)
190. Ibid., p.120.
191. Ibid., p.41.
192. Ibid.
193. Ibid., p.79.
194. Ibid., p.78.
195. Régis Debray, *Christophe Colomb, le visiteur de l'aube* (Paris: La Différence, 1991), p.31.
196. Karl Marx, *A Contribution to the Critique of Political Economy*, in Marx and Engels, *On Literature and Art* (Moscow: Progress Publishers, 1976), p.84.
197. Régis Debray, *Cours de médiologie générale* (Paris: Gallimard, 1991), p.390.
198. Ibid., p.187.
199. Ibid., p.303.
200. Victor Hugo, *Notre-Dame de Paris* (Paris: Livre de Poche, 1966), p.231.
201. Ibid., p.366.
202. Ibid., p.334.
203. Ibid., p.236.
204. Serres, *Éléments de l'histoire des sciences*, p.360.
205. Régis Debray, *Vie et mort de l'image* (Paris: Gallimard, 1992), p.298.
206. Ibid., pp.297–8.
207. Walter Benjamin, *Illuminations* (London: Fontana, 1992), p.232.
208. Debray, *Vie et mort de l'image*, p.174. (The examples given are my own.)
209. Ibid., p.61.
210. Ibid., pp.61–2.
211. Ibid., p.63.
212. Ibid., p.392.
213. Ibid., p.396.
214. Régis Debray, *L'État séducteur* (Paris: Gallimard, 1993), p.192.
215. Ibid.
216. Ibid., p.92.
217. Ibid., p.26.
218. Ibid., p.119.
219. Ibid., p.124.
220. Ibid., p.114.
221. Ibid.
222. Ibid., p.14.
223. Ibid., p.91.
224. Ibid., p.95.

225. Ibid., p.94.
226. Ibid., p.97.
227. Ibid., p.13.
228. Ibid., p.14.
229. Régis Debray, *Un mot encore, cher Beré* (Paris: Arléa, 1993), p.7.
230. Ibid., p.17.
231. Ibid., p.20.
232. Ibid., p.22.
233. Ibid., p.27.
234. Ibid., p.28.
235. Ibid., p.29.
236. Régis Debray, *Manifestes médiologiques* (Paris: Gallimard, 1994), p.186.
237. Ibid., pp.187–8.
238. Ibid., p.198.
239. Ibid., p.12.
240. Ibid., p.23.
241. Ibid., p.38.
242. Ibid., p.87.
243. Ibid., p.104.
244. Ibid., p.141.
245. Ibid., p.152.
246. Ibid., p.163.
247. Régis Debray, *L'Oeil naïf* (Paris: Seuil, 1994), p.7.
248. Ibid., p.9.
249. Ibid., p.10.
250. Ibid., pp.19–20.
251. Ibid., p.20.
252. Ibid., p.31.
253. Ibid., p.32. ('Collaboration' has a capital C in the French.)
254. Ibid., p.34.
255. Ibid., p.32.
256. Ibid., p.59.
257. Ibid., p.93.
258. Ibid., p.100.
259. Ibid., p.98.
260. Ibid., p.99.
261. Ibid., p.129.
262. Ibid., p.168.
263. Ibid., p.174.
264. Ibid., p.184.
265. Ibid., p.183.

Bibliography

This lists all books by Debray, with publisher and date, in chronological order of appearance. Details are provided of English translations where these are or have been available. Newspaper and journal articles, like prefaces and other 'occasional' works, I have felt to be too scattered to be worth including.

There exist (to my knowledge) only two secondary texts solely or extensively devoted to Debray: *Régis Debray and the Latin American Revolution* (New York: Monthly Review Press, 1968), edited by Leo Huberman and Paul M. Sweezy, and Hartmut Ramon's *The Marxism of Régis Debray: Between Lenin and Guevara* (Lawrence: Regents Press of Kansas, 1978).

The place of publication for all French texts is Paris.

La Frontière/Un jeune homme à la page, Seuil, 1967.

Révolution dans la révolution? Maspero, 1967: reprinted with *Autres essais*, Maspero, 1969. (English translation *Revolution in the Revolution?*, trans. B. Ortiz, Harmondsworth: Penguin, 1967.)

Essais sur l'Amérique Latine, Maspero, 1967.

Le Procès de Camiri, Maspero, 1969.

Strategy for Revolution (ed. R. Blackburn), London: Jonathan Cape, 1970.

Entretiens avec Allende sur la situation au Chili, Maspero, 1971.

La Guerrilla du Che, Seuil, 1974. (English translation by Rosemary Sheed, Harmondsworth: Penguin, 1975.)

La Critique des armes, Seuil, 1974. (English translation *The Critique of Arms*, trans. R. Sheed, Harmondsworth: Penguin, 1977).

La Critique des armes 2: Les Épreuves du feu, Seuil, 1974. (English translation *Revolution on Trial*, trans. R. Sheed, Harmondsworth: Penguin, 1978.)

Denain l'Espagne (interviews with Santiago Carrillo by Régis Debray and Max Gallo), Seuil, 1974. (English translation *Dialogue on Spain*, trans. R. Sheed, London: Lawrence and Wishart, 1976.)

Prison Writings (trans. R. Sheed), Harmondsworth: Penguin, 1975.

Les Rendez-Vous Manqués, Seuil, 1975.

L'Indésirable, Seuil, 1975. (English translation *Undesirable Alien*, trans. R. Sheed, Harmondsworth: Allen Lane, 1978.)

Journal d'un petit bourgeois entre deux feux et quatre murs, Seuil, 1976.
La Neige brûle, Grasset, 1977.
Lettres aux communistes français et à quelques autres, Seuil, 1978.
Modeste contribution aux discours et cérémonies officielles du dixième anniversaire, Maspero, 1978. (English translation in *New Left Review*, no.115, 1979.)
Le Pouvoir intellectuel en France, Ramsay, 1979/Gallimard Folio, 1989. (English translation *Teachers, Writers, Celebrities*, trans. D. Macey, London: New Left Books, 1981.)
Le Scribe, Grasset, 1980.
Critique de la raison politique, Gallimard, 1981. (English translation *Critique of Political Reason*, trans. D. Macey, London: Verso/New Left Books, 1983.)
La Puissance et les rêves, Gallimard, 1984.
Les Empires contre l'europe, Gallimard, 1985.
Éloges, Gallimard, 1986.
Comète, ma comète, Gallimard, 1986.
Les Masques, Gallimard, 1987.
Tous azimuts, Odile Jacob, 1989.
Que vive la République!, Odile Jacob, 1989.
A demain de Gaulle!, Gallimard, 1990. (English translation *Charles de Gaulle: Futurist of the Nation*, trans. J. Howe, London: Verso/New Left Books, 1994.)
Christophe Colomb, le visiteur de l'aube, La Différence, 1991.
Cours de médiologie générale, Gallimard, 1991.
Vie et mort de l'image, Gallimard, 1992.
L'État séducteur, Gallimard, 1993.
Un mot encore, cher Béré, Arléa, 1993.
(with Jean Ziegler) *Il s'agit de ne pas se rendre*, Arléa, 1994.
Manifestes médiologiques, Gallimard, 1994.
L'Oeil naïf, Seuil, 1994.

Index

Index by Auriol Griffith-Jones